What People are Saying About Bible Praying for Parents

"You want the very best God has for your child, right? Then don't miss out on this easy-to-use guide. Every parent who is passionate about joining biblical wisdom with heart-felt prayers for their child can invest just a minute a day with this book and reap a lifetime of reward. Genius!"

~Les Parrott, Ph.D., #1 New York Times bestselling author of Saving Your Marriage Before It Starts

"Many Christian parents are looking for ways to help energize their kid's faith. This book is a simple, natural way to pray together and have faith conversations as a family. Keeping it short and practical while planting the Word of God in their hearts is a beautiful way to help your family grow. I wholeheartedly recommend this book."

~Jim Burns, PhD, Dad, Grandfather, President, HomeWord, author of Faith Conversations for Families *and* The Purity Code.

"Keith and Judy have provided one of the most practical resources for parents who want to spiritually impact their children. And - it's ALL based solely on God's Word. Praying these scriptures over your children will change their lives for eternity!"

~Brian Dollar, Dad, author of Talk Now And Later: How To Lead Kids Through Life's Tough Topics, *and blogger at BrianDollar.com*

"I have been praying the Scriptures on and off for my own children for years. However, Bible Praying for Parents takes praying the scriptures over my children to a whole new level. This is a resource I not only NEED but a resource I will USE. Keith and Judy provide a system of organization and clarity, making it easy to jump in, start today and have a clear path. I highly recommend this resource and am excited to see this concept laid out so easily and thoughtfully for parents who want to make an eternal difference in their own children. Bible Praying for Parents will impact my children and I pray it finds its way into thousands of homes."

~Josh Denhart KidMin Science; The Amazing Chemistry Show; Science VBS

"I love this resource! There are few greater expressions of love than to pray for someone, but it's so easy to get into prayer ruts. Bible Praying for Parents gives me hundreds of ways to pray with and for my kids. And best of all, they're straight from the heart of God!"

~David Rausch, Dad, CEO of Mooblio.org and creator of the Go! Curriculum

"As a mom of four, Bible Praying for Parents will immediately be put to use in my home. This may be the most practical parenting book I have seen, from the first prayer to the blessings, any parent can begin directed, purposeful prayers for their children which are straight from the Word of God. I am excited to see how Keith's and Judy's work to equip parents will change generations to come!"

~Courtney Wilson, Mom, Elementary Pastor at Christ Community Church (Chicago)

"Bible Praying for Parents is a powerful tool in the hands of a powerful God. I can only imagine what God will do in the lives of the next generation. As a pastor of children and youth for over 30 years, this is a resource I want to equip parents to use and pray over their children. As a father of four I will be using this to pray over my children...and someday my grandchildren!"

~Tom Bump, Husband, Dad, Kids Pastor and Coach to Parents and Ministry Leaders

"This is an amazing resource not only for parents, but for anyone who has a relationship with a child. With this book, the daily discipline of prayer can quickly become a reality. Praying Scripture with and over your children daily will change their lives and models a healthy pattern of prayer for their own life. God provided the words for us to use, and Keith and Judy brought them to us in an accessible, organized way. This book is a must for your parenting arsenal!"

~Tracy Baer, Mom of grown kids, and Events Director at International Network of Children's Ministry

"Practical, intentional, and timely. This book should be a 'go to' for every parent as they strive to raise men and women who love Jesus. It's beautiful."

~Melissa J. MacDonald, Ministry Innovator, Children's Disciplemaking Specialist for The Christian and Missionary Alliance

"If you have kids in your life - young or old, family or friends - who you care about and want to see live as passionate disciples of Jesus Christ, praying Scripture with and for them is vital and powerful. Bible Praying for Parents gives clear, concise prayers anyone can EASILY work into their daily routine. The best books on prayer are ones that actually help us pray more faithfully and effectively. Bible Praying for Parents does exactly that. This book wonderfully combines three vital elements of leading kids to walk with Jesus: prayer, Scripture and consistency. Utilizing this book is one of the best gifts you can give to the kids in your life."

~Randy Isola, Dad, Children's Pastor at Christ Community Church (Chicago, IL)

"When we pray God's words back to Him on behalf of our children (or grandchildren), we can have confidence our prayers are consistent with God's desires. Bible Praying for Parents gives you the structure and helps with the discipline needed to pray this way regularly and consistently on behalf of your family members!"

~Larry Fowler, Founder, The Legacy Coalition

"All of Jesus' words on prayer could be put into one word: Ask! Bible Praying for Parents provides God's Words to be spoken by parents as "prayers for the asking." Use this book to pray a daily Word from Scripture for your child, personalizing it with their name, or pray God's Word to focus on a spiritual area or to bless them. Keith and Judy have provided parents with a ready-made, practical, simple, yet powerful daily prayer guide that will transform the hearts and minds of our children and the parents praying God's Word for them."

~Jane Kriel Horn, Worship & Arts Minister, St. Michael's Lutheran Church, Bloomington, MN

"We LOVE this book! Keith and Judy make it possible for simple, yet powerful, moments each day to pray scripture specifically over our children. The daily verses, topics, and prayers make this book practical to use - and something we look forward to incorporating into each and every morning!"

~David and Teesha Laflin, Dad and Mom, internationally recognized illusionists and entrepreneurs, DavidAndTeesha.com

"Prayer works! Keith and Judy have created the perfect guide for parents and grandparents who want to be intentional about praying for children. I wish they would have written this book sooner!"

~Ryan Frank, Dad, CEO/Publisher, KidzMatter

"Most parents pray for their kids, but many don't know exactly what to pray day-to-day. Bible Praying for Parents gives a simple practical way to pray through every area of your kids' lives over a year. You're in the Word. You're praying the Word over them. A huge win-win!"

~*Jonathan McKee, author of* If I Had Parenting Do Over *and* The Teens Guide to Social Media and Mobile Devices

"A parent's influence on his or her child is exponential and often invisible. While prayers at meals and bedtime matter, Keith and Judy know there's something special about moms and dads praying consistently and specifically for their kids behind-the-scenes. Bible Praying for Kids is a refreshingly practical resource that engages parents with God's Word as they lift their children up to Him."

~*Dan Lovaglia, Dad, Author of Relational Children's Ministry*

"Love, love, love this book! The first scripture that came to my mind after reading this life-giving book was, "Teach me to number my days so that I may gain a heart of wisdom." (Psalm 90:12) This intentional and simplified approach for pausing before the Lord each day and praying for our children is amazing! This would make a great baby dedication gift and/or milestone ministry gift."

~*Stephanie Porter, Children's Ministry Pastor, Orange Specialist/ Orange Coaching*

"Keith and Judy have focused this book in such a practical way on a very foundational spiritual discipline. In my observation and from my own personal experience in our fast-paced, "crazy busy" world in which we live, it can be a real struggle to be consistent in prayer. Using God's Word as a launching point to pray for specific areas of our children's lives is not only simple and doable but also profound and transformational. I plan to purchase this book for my women's ministry leaders."

~*Michele Jancola, Mom, and Women's Ministry Director at Highlands Community Church*

"Bible Praying for Parents should be in the hands of every parent or guardian. Regardless of the age and stage of their children, this incredible book is a remarkable guide to praying the words of God over our children's lives. Not only that, but it is a daily, beautiful reminder that the truths of Scripture are transformative and powerful... a welcome reminder to any parent who is committed to the discipleship of their kids."

~*Michayla White, Mom, and Associate Director at International Network of Children's Ministry*

Bible Praying
For Parents

Keith Ferrin
Judy Fetzer

Bible Praying for Parents
© 2017 Keith Ferrin All Rights Reserved
Published June 18, 2017 by Keith Ferrin Productions, LLC

ISBN: 0-9740023-5-6 (print)
        0-9740023-6-4 (eBook)

Contact the publisher at:
KeithFerrin.com, info@KeithFerrin.com

Book Cover Design: Brian Gage, Pipe & Tabor, Vancouver, WA
Interior Design: Alane Pearce Professional Writing Services, LLC, Baltimore, MD

Table of Contents

Dedication   9
A Note from Judy   10
A Note from Keith   11

Section 1 Bible Praying Day by Day   **13**
January   15
February   31
March   47
April   63
May   79
June   95
July   111
August   127
September   143
October   159
November   175
December   191

Section 2 Bible Praying by Category   **207**
Anger   211
Anxiety   213
Blessing   216
Character   220
Church   228
Faith   229
Faithful Living   231
Family   235
Friendship   237
Future   241
Heart   244
Life Issues   246
Love God's Word   248
Mind and Body   251
Missions   253

Others   255
Praise   260
Prodigal   262
Protection   264
School   265
Service   267
Soul   269
Temptation   274
Thanks   279
Work Ethic   280

Section 3 Bible Blessings   **281**

About the Authors   **297**

Dedication

This book is dedicated to Sarah, Caleb, and Hannah. May these prayers I am praying over the three of you be prayed over your children someday…and their children someday…and their children… ~*Keith*

To Melissa, thank you for the many years we prayed together — we were blessed to see God answer our many petitions. I'm grateful for all you showed me: a passion for prayer, a deep belief in power of Christ's work in our lives, and the value of praising God before bringing our list to Him. It changed me and it changed our children's lives. ~*Judy*

A Note from Judy

As a young mom with young kids in elementary school, there was a lot to worry about. Knowing I was sending my precious, tender-hearted children into public school only added to my concern. And then I met Melissa. Her fervor and belief in prayer inspired me; my knowledge of finding Scripture in the Bible inspired her. Together, when we two moms prayed God's word over our children, specifically and Biblically; we found comfort, support, and peace that only comes from resting in Christ. By joining together, inviting God into our concerns and opening His word, we could rest, knowing that God's word was at work on the school grounds, in the classroom, in the staff and administrators at school.

During my children's middle school years, I returned to college and was alarmed by the culture. I knew the struggles my kids would soon come against as they entered college and wanted to continue to pray daily for them using God's Word. But like most of us, I often forgot to pray -- I meant to set aside time but life is busy with three kids. One day while reading a blog I realized I could put the Scripture prayers I'd collected through the years onto my own blog and send them to myself by email. When I checked my email every day, there would be a reminder to pray. I invited other mom's to subscribe, to find the same comfort and peace from God's word, and that's how my humble little ministry was born[1].

I invite you to begin your time of prayer with Scripture. Pray it over those God brings to your mind. Then rest, knowing God is at work.

Judy Fetzer

---

[1] *You can follow my ministry blog here: www.mamahenprays.wordpress.com*

A Note from Keith

When Judy told me about her blog of "daily Bible prayers," I thought it sounded interesting. So...I went to the blog and signed up to receive the updates. What I didn't expect was to have Judy's simple, daily blog transform the way I pray for my own kids!

Simple prayers. Profound prayers. Bible prayers. Praying the actual words of Scripture for my kids, over my kids, and sometimes with my kids. Every day.

I was hooked. I also found myself reading the Bible and noticing other verses I could add to the list. Sometimes I would jot them down. Sometimes I would stop and pray the verses right then. Sometimes I would write them on a notecard and tape them to their bathroom mirror. And sometimes I would pray them out loud over them as they ate their breakfast and got ready for school.

When I approached Judy about turning these prayers into a book, I was grateful she agreed. We've added a section with the prayers organized by category and another section with Bible "blessings" you can pray in the mornings, at bedtime, at meals, or anytime.

I partnered with Judy to write this book because I need it. We are sharing it with you in the hope, prayer, and belief that God will use it to transform the frequency, enjoyment, and impact of your own prayers for your children.

Bible praying for your kids and mine,

Keith Ferrin

Section 1
Bible Praying Day by Day

January

God calls us to pray without ceasing, so you can have confidence as you approach God's throne that your prayers are powerful and they will be heard by God.

January 1

Category: Character
Verse: Psalm 25:21
Focus: Pray for your child's school year.

May integrity and uprightness protect _____, may his(her) hope be in You. ~Amen (Psalm 25:21)

NOTES:

January 2

Category: Others
Verse: Mark 12:30-31
Focus: Pray for your child's devotion to God / to love God.

May _____ love You Lord God, with all of his(her) heart, all of his(her) soul, all of his(her) mind, and all of his(her) strength. And let _____ love his(her) neighbor as himself(herself), because there is no commandment greater than these. ~Amen (Mark 12:30-31 NLT)

NOTES:

January 3

Category: Others
Verse: Philippians 2:3-4
Focus: Pray for your child to have a humble spirit /be unselfish / exhibit humility.

Lord God, help _____ not be selfish or live to make a good impression on others. Instead let _____ be humble, thinking of others as better than himself(herself). May _____ not think only about his(her) own affairs, but be interested in others too, and what they are doing. ~Amen (Philippians 2:3-4 NLT)

NOTES:

January 4

Category: Family
Verse: Psalm 133:1
Focus: Pray for family harmony.

Lord, help each one in our family make our home a wonderful and pleasant place where brothers (and sisters) live together in harmony! ~Amen (Psalm 133:1 NLT)

NOTES:

January 5

Category: Love God's Word
Verse: Colossians 2:7
Focus: Pray for your child's spiritual growth.

Heavenly Father, let _____'s roots grow down into You, Lord, and draw up nourishment from Christ, so he(she) will grow in faith, strong and vigorous in the truth. Let _____'s life overflow with thanksgiving for all He has done. ~Amen (Colossians 2:7 NLT)

NOTES:

January 6

Category: Character
Verse: Psalm 139:4, 12
Focus: Pray for your child's path / heart.

Holy Father, You know what _____ is going to say even before he(she) says it. Shine Your light on the darkness of _____'s life so he(she) cannot hide from You. Search _____ and know his(her) heart...lead him(her) in the path of everlasting life. ~Amen (Psalm 139:4, 12 NLT)

NOTES:

January 7

Category: Heart
Verse: Psalm 51:17
Focus: Pray for a repentant heart for your child.

Dear Lord, show _____ that the sacrifice You want, O God, is a broken spirit; a broken and repentant heart You will not despise. ~Amen (Psalm 51:17 NLT)

NOTES:

January 8

Category: Friendship
Verse: Proverbs 12:17
Focus: Pray for your child's word choices.

Heavenly Father, help _____ be an honest witness who tells the truth. Help him(her) not be a person who makes cutting remarks, instead give him(her) words of wisdom that bring healing. ~Amen (Proverbs 12:17 NLT)

NOTES:

January 9

Category: Future
Verse: Psalm 61:6-7
Focus: Pray for your child's future.

Dear Lord, I pray that You would add many years to _____'s life; may Your unfailing love and faithfulness watch over him(her). ~Amen (Psalm 61:7 NLT)

NOTES:

January 10

Category: Anger
Verse: Colossians 3:8-10
Focus: Pray for your child's character.

Gracious God, may _____ get rid of any anger or rage in his(her) life, help _____ also get rid of any malicious behavior, slander, or dirty language. Don't let _____ lie to others; instead may _____ clothe himself(herself) with a brand new nature that is continually being renewed as he(she) learns more and more about You Christ, who created this new nature within _____. ~Amen
(Colossians 3:8-10 NLT)

NOTES:

January 11

Category: Work Ethic
Verse: Colossians 3:23-24
Focus: Pray for your child's work ethic.

Holy Father, may _____ work willingly at whatever he(she) does, as though working for the Lord rather than for people. Help _____ remember that the Master he(she) is serving is Christ. ~Amen
(Colossians 3:23-24 NLT)

NOTES:

January 12

Category: Missions
Verse: Matthew 5:16
Focus: Pray for your child to shine.

Gracious God, May _____'s good deeds shine out for all to see, so that everyone will praise You, Heavenly Father. ~Amen (Matthew 5:16 NLT)

NOTES:

January 13

Category: Character
Verse: Colossians 1:9-10
Focus: Pray for your child's life to honor God.

God, I ask that You give _____ complete knowledge of Your will, as well as spiritual wisdom and understanding. May the way _____ lives always be honoring and pleasing to You, Lord. May _____'s life produce every kind of good fruit, and may he(she) grow and learn to know You better and better, God. ~Amen (Colossians 1:9-10 NLT)

NOTES:

January 14

Category: Others/Service
Verse: Galatians 6:9-10
Focus: Pray for your child to do the right thing / persevere.

Lord God, may _____ not get tired of doing what is good. Remind him(her) that at just the right time he(she) will reap a harvest of blessing if he(she) doesn't give up. Whenever _____ has the opportunity, let him(her) do good to everyone—especially to those in the family of faith. ~Amen (Galatians 6:9-10 NLT)

NOTES:

January 15

Category: Church
Verse: Matthew 18:20
Focus: Pray for your child to enjoy church fellowship.

Heavenly Father, remind _____ of the importance of meeting together with other believers, for where two or more gather together as Christ's followers, You are there among them. ~Amen (Matthew 18:20 NLT)

NOTES:

January 16

Category: Character
Verse: Colossians 3:12-14
Focus: Pray for your child's heart / family harmony.

Dear Lord, would You clothe _____ with tenderhearted
mercy, with kindness, with humility, with gentleness, and with
patience. May _____ forgive anyone who offends him(her),
remembering that You, Lord, forgave him(her). Above all, clothe
_____ with love, which binds us all together in perfect harmony.
~Amen (Colossians 3:12-14)

NOTES:

January 17

Category: Temptation
Verse: Hebrews 12:10-11
Focus: Pray for your child's self discipline.

Lord God, thank You for disciplining _____ so that he(she) might
share in Your holiness. Use this discipline, which is not enjoyable
while it is happening but painful to grow _____ in his(her)
character and produce a peaceful harvest of right living. ~Amen
(Hebrews 12:10-11 NLT)

NOTES:

January 18

Category: Missions
Verse: Psalm 96:3
Focus: Pray for your child to reveal God's glory.

Heavenly Father, I pray that You would help _____ develop
a desire to see Your glory declared among the nations, Your
marvelous works among all peoples. ~Amen (Psalm 96:3 ESV)

NOTES:

January 19

Category: Temptation
Verse: Romans 16:19
Focus: Pray for wisdom for your child.

Heavenly Father, may _____ be wise as to what is good and
innocent as to what is evil. ~Amen (Romans 16:19 ESV)

NOTES:

January 20

Category: Future
Verse: 3 John 2
Focus: Pray a blessing over your child's life.

Lord God, I pray that _____ would have good fortune in everything he(she) does. May _____ be in good health, and may his(her) everyday affairs prosper, as well as his(her) soul. ~Amen (3 John 2, MSG)

NOTES:

January 21

Category: Prodigal
Verse: Psalm 121:7-8
Focus: Pray for protection over your child.

Lord, I ask that You would keep all harm from _____ and watch over his(her) life. Keep watch, Lord, over _____ as he(she) comes and goes, both now and forevermore. ~Amen (Psalm 121:7-8)

NOTES:

January 22

Category: Anxiety
Verse: Romans 8:31
Focus: Pray for your child when you're worried.

Gracious God, I pray that You would remind _____ that if You are for him(her), who can be against him(her)? ~Amen
(Romans 8:31)

NOTES:

January 23

Category: Soul
Verse: John 14:6
Focus: Pray for your child's soul.

Heavenly Father, may _____ know You, Lord, as the Way, the Truth, and the Life. Build his(her) faith to know that no one comes to the Father except through Christ. ~Amen
(John 14:6 NLT)

NOTES:

January 24

Category: Faithful Living
Verse: Proverbs 24:5-6
Focus: Pray for your child to have a mentor / wisdom for your child.

Lord, give _____ wisdom in all things because the wise are mightier than the strong, and those with knowledge grow stronger and stronger. May _____ seek wise guidance since victory depends on having advisers. ~Amen (Proverbs 24:5-6)

NOTES:

January 25

Category: Character
Verse: John 15:12
Focus: Pray for your children's relationships / sibling relationships.

God, help _____ follow Your commandment to love each other the way You have loved him(her), especially his(her) siblings, give them a loving bond. ~Amen (John 15:12 NLT)

NOTES:

January 26

Category: Character
Verse: 2 Peter 1:5-7
Focus: Pray for your child's morals / character.

Lord, may _____ make every effort to respond
to Your promises. Supplement his(her) faith with a generous
provision of moral excellence; along with moral excellence, give
_____ knowledge, self-control, patient endurance, godliness,
brotherly affection and love for everyone. ~Amen
(2 Peter 1:5-7 NLT)

NOTES:

January 27

Category: Friendship
Verse: Proverbs 17:17, Proverbs 18:24
Focus: Pray for your child to be a good friend and have good
friendships.

Dear God, as iron sharpens iron, surround _____ with friends
that will sharpen him(her) as a friend. May _____ be a real friend
that sticks closer than a brother. ~Amen
(Proverbs 17:17, Proverbs 18:24)

NOTES:

January 28

Category: Love God's Word
Verse: Isaiah 40:25-26
Focus: Pray for your child to know the creator.

Wonderful God, May _____ know You as the God who has no equal, none compare with You. When _____ looks up into the heavens, remind him(her) that You created all the stars, You bring them out like an army, one after another, calling each by its name; because of Your great power and incomparable strength, not a single one is missing. Reveal Yourself to _____. ~Amen (Isaiah 40:25-26 NLT)

NOTES:

January 29

Category: Character
Verse: Hebrews 12:1
Focus: Pray for you child to live life well / child's faith.

Dear Lord, You have surrounded us with a huge crowd of witnesses to the life of faith; let _____ strip off every weight that slows him(her) down, especially the sin that so easily trips him(her) up. And let _____ run with endurance the race You, God, has set before him(her). ~Amen (Hebrews 12:1 NLT)

NOTES:

January 30

Category: Love God's Word
Verse: Jeremiah 15:16
Focus: Pray for your child to enjoy God's Word / love God's Word.

Gracious God, help _____ discover Your Words and devour them. May Your Words be _____'s joy and his(her) heart's delight; may _____ bear Your name, O Lord God of Heaven's Armies. ~Amen (Jeremiah 15:16 NLT)

NOTES:

January 31

Category: Soul
Verse: 1 Thessalonians 5:23-24
Focus: Pray for your child's spirit.

Heavenly Father, You are the God of peace. Make _____ holy in every way. May his(her) whole spirit and soul and body be kept blameless until our Lord Jesus Christ comes again. Remind _____ that You are faithful. ~Amen (1 Thessalonians 5:23-24 NLT)

NOTES:

February

Prayer is a powerful tool to bring your worries to the throne of God. Remember as you pray that He hears you and offers you peace.

February 1

Category: Blessing
Verse: Psalm 40:11
Focus: Pray for your child to know God's love.

Lord, I pray that You will not withhold Your compassion from _____; that Your loving-kindness and Your truth will continually preserve _____. ~Amen (Psalm 40:11 NASB)

NOTES:

February 2

Category: Soul
Verse: Hosea 11
Focus: Pray for your prodigal child.

Gracious God, when _____ was a child, You loved him(her). You led _____ along with Your ropes of kindness and love. But _____ right now is refusing to return to You; he(she) seems determined to desert You. Though he(she) is tearing at Your heart, continue to let Your compassion flow over him(her). Bring _____ home again. ~Amen (Hosea 11: 1, 4, 5, 7, 11 NLT)

NOTES:

February 3

Category: Temptation
Verse: Ephesians 5:10-14
Focus: Pray for your child to be transparent.

Heavenly Father, may _____ carefully determine what pleases You, Lord. Block him(her) from taking part in the worthless deeds of evil and darkness; instead expose them. Shine Your light on any evil intentions of _____'s mind and expose them. Your light makes everything visible. ~Amen (Ephesians 5:10-14)

NOTES:

February 4

Category: Temptation
Verse: Titus 2:11-12
Focus: Pray for your child's righteousness.

God of Grace, reveal Your grace to _____. I pray that he(she) would do as Your Word instructs and turn from godless living and sinful pleasures. May _____ live in this evil world with wisdom, righteousness, and devotion to You, God. ~Amen (Titus 2:11 -12 NLT)

NOTES:

February 5

Category: Blessing
Verse: Romans 15:13
Focus: Pray for your child at school.

I pray that You, the God of hope, would fill _____ with all joy and peace as he(she) trusts in You, so that _____ may overflow with hope by the power of the Holy Spirit. ~Amen (Romans 15:13)

NOTES:

February 6

Category: Life Issues
Verse: Ephesians 5:18
Focus: Pray for your child's choices.

O God, Don't let _____ be drunk with wine (or alcohol), because it may ruin his(her) life. Instead may _____ be filled with the Holy Spirit. ~Amen (Ephesians 5:18 NLT)

NOTES:

February 7

Category: Life Issues
Verse: Proverbs 2:1-3
Focus: Pray for your child's music choices.

Lord, may _____ listen to what You say and treasure Your commands. When he(she) tunes into music, tune his(her) ear to wisdom, help him(her) concentrate on the lyrics and cry out for insight and ask for understanding as to music choices. ~Amen (Proverbs 2:1-3 NLT)

NOTES:

February 8

Category: Mind and Body
Verse: 1 Samuel 16:7
Focus: Pray for your child's self esteem.

Gracious God, I pray that You would remind _____ that You see him(her) through Your eyes; You don't see his(her) appearance, You see _____'s heart. ~Amen (1 Samuel 16:7)

NOTES:

February 9

Category: Friendship
Verse: Proverbs 22:24-25
Focus: Pray for your child's discernment with friends.

Dear Lord, help _____ not befriend angry people or associate with hot-tempered people, keep him(her) from learning to be like them and endangering his(her) own soul. ~Amen
(Proverbs 22:24-25 NLT)

NOTES:

February 10

Category: Anxiety
Verse: Romans 8:35-39
Focus: Pray for your child to know God's love.

Dear God, don't let anything separate _____ from Christ's love. Thank You that You love _____ even if he(she) is in trouble or experiences calamity, even if he(she) is persecuted or hungry or destitute or in danger or threatened with death, nothing can separate _____ from Your love, O God. Remind him(her) not to fear today or worry about tomorrow because he(she) has overwhelming victory through Christ. ~Amen (Romans 8:35-39 NLT)

NOTES:

February 11

Category: Future
Verse: Jeremiah 29:11-13
Focus: Pray for your child's future.

You know, O Lord, the plans You have for _____, plans for good and not for disaster, to give him(her) a future and a hope. May _____ pray to You, and listen for You, may he(she) look for You, God, in earnest; You have promised to find _____ when he(she) seeks You. ~Amen (Jeremiah 29:11-13 NLT)

NOTES:

February 12

Category: Future
Verse: 2 Corinthians 6:14-17
Focus: Pray for your child's dating.

Dear God, when _____ dates, may he(she) not team up with those who are unbelievers. May _____ see that goodness cannot partner with wickedness, and light cannot live with darkness. Remind _____ that he(she) is a temple of the living God. ~Amen (2 Corinthians 6:14-17 NLT)

NOTES:

February 13

Category: Anxiety
Verse: Joshua 1:9
Focus: Pray for your child to be courageous when he(she) is afraid.

Heavenly Father, Enable _____ to be strong and very courageous. Be with him(her) when he(she) is afraid or discouraged and remind him(her) that You are with him(her) wherever he(she) goes. ~Amen (Joshua 1:9 NLT)

NOTES:

February 14

Category: Others
Verse: 2 Corinthians 9:6-8
Focus: Pray for your child's money management.

Lord God, teach _____ to sow generously so that he(she) might reap generously. Guide him(her) in how much he(she) should give. May _____ not give reluctantly or in response to pressure; let him(her) be a person who loves You and gives cheerfully. ~Amen (2 Corinthians 9:6-8 NLT)

NOTES:

February 15

Category: Life Issues
Verse: 2 Samuel 22:31
Focus: Pray for your child to trust God.

Dear Lord, show _____ that Your way, God, is perfect, that Your Word is proven. Be _____'s shield as he(she) trusts in You. ~Amen (2 Samuel 22:31 NLT)

NOTES:

February 16

Category: Future
Verse: Romans 12:6-8
Focus: Pray for your child's spiritual gifts.

Lord, You have given each of us different gifts, help _____ to use the gifts You've given; whether it be ministering, teaching, exhorting/encouraging, may he(she) do it well. If You've gifted _____ to give, may he(she) give liberally; if the gift is leading, may he(she) lead with diligence; if the gift is showing mercy, may he(she) give mercy cheerfully. ~Amen. (Romans 12:6-8 NLT)

NOTES:

February 17

Category: Character
Verse: Psalm 90:14
Focus: Pray for your child to know God's love.

I pray heavenly Father, that _____ would be satisfied in the morning, with Your steadfast love. May he(she) rejoice and be glad all of his(her) days. ~Amen (Psalm 90:14 ESV)

NOTES:

February 18

Category: Love God's Word
Verse: Psalm 33:4
Focus: Pray for your child to read the Bible and know God.

Lord, I pray that _____ will know that Your Word is right and true, and that he(she) can know You are faithful in all You do. ~Amen (Psalm 33:4 NLT)

NOTES:

February 19

Category: Love God's Word
Verse: Luke 24:45
Focus: Pray for Biblical wisdom for your child.

Lord God, I pray that You would open _____'s mind so that he(she) can understand the Scriptures. ~Amen (Luke 24:45)

NOTES:

February 20

Category: Prodigal
Verse: Psalm 63:7-8
Focus: Pray for God's protection over your child.

Good and gracious God, remind _____ how much You have
helped him(her); may _____ sing for joy in the shadow of Your
protecting wings. Follow close behind _____, I praise You that
Your right hand holds _____ securely. ~Amen (Psalm 63:7-8 NLT)

NOTES:

February 21

Category: Faithful Living
Verse: 1 John 5:14
Focus: Pray for your child's confidence in God.

Gracious God, I pray that You would give _____ confidence as
he(she) approaches You; help him(her) know that if he(she) asks
anything according to Your will, You hear. ~Amen (1 John 5:14)

NOTES:

February 22

Category: Integrity
Verse: 1 Corinthians 6:12
Focus: Pray for your child's reasoning skills.

Dear Lord, help _____ to know that just because something is technically legal doesn't mean it is spiritually appropriate. ~Amen (1 Corinthians 6:12 MSG)

NOTES:

February 23

Category: Family
Verse: Romans 15:5, 7
Focus: Pray for family harmony.

God, would You give _____ patience and encouragement; help him(her) live in complete harmony with his(her) siblings, as is fitting for followers of Christ Jesus. Help _____ to accept others just as Christ has accepted him(her), so that You, God, will be given glory. ~Amen (Romans 15:5, 7 NLT)

NOTES:

February 24

Category: Faithful Living
Verse: 1 Corinthians 15:58
Focus: Pray for your child's faith.

Dear God, I pray during _____'s life, he(she) would be strong and immovable, always working enthusiastically for You Lord, knowing that nothing he(she) does for You is ever useless. ~Amen
(1 Corinthians 15:58 NLT)

NOTES:

February 25

Category: Parent/Child Relationship
Verse: Ephesians 6:4
Focus: Pray for how you parent your child.

Lord, as parents, help us not provoke _____ to anger by the way we treat them. Rather, help us bring up_____ with the discipline and instruction that comes from You, Lord. ~Amen
(Ephesians 6:4 NLT)

NOTES:

February 26

Category: Future
Verse: Philippians 3:13-14
Focus: Pray for your child to be confident in the future.

Dear Lord, I pray that _____ would forget the past and look forward to what lies ahead, help him(her) press on to reach the end of the race and receive the heavenly prize for which God, through Christ Jesus, is calling him(her). ~Amen (Philippians 3:13-14 NLT)

NOTES:

February 27

Category: Soul
Verse: Hebrews 4:12
Focus: Pray for your child's heart.

Your word, O God, is living and active, sharper than any double-edged sword, use it in _____'s life to penetrate to his(her) soul and spirit, joints and marrow; help _____ apply your word to judge the thoughts and attitudes of his(her) heart. ~Amen (Hebrews 4:12)

NOTES:

February 28

Category: Integrity
Verse: 1 Corinthians 16:13
Focus: Pray for your child's inner strength.

Dear Lord, help _____ to be on guard, to stand firm in his(her) faith, to be a man(woman) of courage, and to be strong. Above all, help _____ do everything out of love. ~Amen
(1 Corinthians 16:13 NIV)

NOTES:

March

A prayer from the heart of faith is powerful and faith-infused intercession. Be confident that praying in faith moves the heart of God.

March 1

Category: School
Verse: 2 Corinthians 5:7
Focus: Pray for your child's teacher.

Dear God, may _____ be a person who walks by faith and not by sight. ~Amen (2 Corinthians 5:7)

NOTES:

March 2

Category: Others
Verse: Luke 6:27-31
Focus: Pray for your child to have a giving spirit and to be generous.

Holy God, may _____ listen to Your words and do good to those who oppose You, God. May he(she) pray for happiness for all those around him(her). Help _____ give what he(she) has to anyone who asks for it, and do for others what he(she) would like them to do for him(her). ~Amen (Luke 6:27-31 NLT)

NOTES:

March 3

Category: Soul
Verse: 2 Corinthians 4:4-6
Focus: Pray for your child to trust God.

Heavenly Father, remove the veil from _____ so he(she) is able to see the glorious life of the Good News that is shining upon him(her). Help _____ understand the message about the glory of Christ. ~Amen (2 Corinthians 4:4-6 NLT)

NOTES:

March 4

Category: Future
Verse: 2 Samuel 22:31
Focus: Pray for your child to trust God.

Dear Lord, show _____ that Your way, God, is perfect, that Your Word is proven. Be _____'s shield as he(she) trusts in You. ~Amen (2 Samuel 22:31 NLT)

NOTES:

March 5

Category: Soul
Verse: Romans 12:2
Focus: Pray for your child to know God's will.

Father God, may _____ not copy the behavior and customs of this world, instead, God, would You transform him(her) into a new person by changing the ways he(she) thinks. Help _____ know what You want him(her) to do, so that he(she) will know Your good and pleasing and perfect will. ~Amen (Romans 12:2 NLT)

NOTES:

March 6

Category: Faithful Living
Verse: 1 Peter 2:11-12
Focus: Pray for your child to live for God.

Dear Lord, I pray that You help _____ remember this world is not his(her) home and not let him(her)self get too cozy in it, indulging his(her) ego at the sake of his(her) soul. May _____ live an exemplary life so that his(her) actions will win others over to God's side and be there to join in the celebration when Christ arrives. ~Amen (1 Corinthians 15:58 MSG)

NOTES:

March 7

Category: Character
Verse: Ephesians 6:18
Focus: Pray for your child to be prayerful.

Dear Lord, I pray _____ would grow into a person that prays hard and long, prays for his(her) brothers, sisters, and fellow believers. Help _____ keep his(her) eyes open and keep each other's spirits up so that no one falls behind or drops out. ~Amen (Ephesians 6:18 MSG)

NOTES:

March 8

Category: Character
Verse: 1 Corinthians 13:4-7
Focus: Pray for your child to be loving, patient, and kind.

Just as You are loving Lord, cause _____ to be loving, to be patient and kind. May _____ not be jealous or boastful or proud or rude. May _____ never demand his(her) own way, be irritable, or keep a record when he(she) has been wronged. May _____ never be glad about injustice but rejoice whenever the truth wins out. May _____ both know and give love that never gives up, never loses faith, remains hopeful and endures through every circumstance. ~Amen (1 Corinthians 13:4-7 NLT)

NOTES:

March 9

Category: School
Verse: Hebrews 13:17-18
Focus: Pray for your child to be respectful.

Gracious God, cause _____ to obey his(her) leaders. Remind him(her) that they are accountable to You, God, and that he(she) should pray for them to live honorably. ~Amen
(Hebrews 13:17-18 NLT)

NOTES:

March 10

Category: Missions
Verse: Matthew 28:19-20
Focus: Pray for your child to be a leader in missions.

Heavenly Father, I pray that _____ would go and make disciples of all nations, baptizing them in the name of the Father and the Son and the Holy Spirit. Help _____ teach these new disciples to obey all of Your commands; remind _____ that You are always with him(her), even to the end of the age. ~Amen (Matthew 28:19-20 NLT)

NOTES:

March 11

Category: Character
Verse: James 1:2-4
Focus: Pray for your child's faith.

Lord God, when trouble comes _____'s way, help him(her) see it as an opportunity for joy. When _____'s faith is tested, may his(her) endurance grow so that he(she) will be strong in character and ready for anything. ~Amen (James 1:2-4 NLT)

NOTES:

March 12

Category: Character
Verse: James 1:3-5
Focus: Pray for your child's confidence.

Heavenly Father, when _____ needs wisdom, remind him(her) to ask You, God, for You will gladly give it and not resent his(her) asking. May _____ fully expect You to answer and not have a doubtful mind that is driven and tossed by the wind. ~Amen (James 1:5-6 NLT)

NOTES:

March 13

Category: Praise
Verse: Psalm 100:2-3
Focus: Pray for your child to worship God / enjoy worshipping God.

Gracious God, may _____ worship You, Lord, with gladness. May he(she) come before You, singing with joy and acknowledge that You are the Lord God. You made ___ and he(she) is one of Yours. ~Amen (Psalm 100:2-3 NLT)

NOTES:

March 14

Category: Temptation
Verse: Acts 3:20
Focus: Pray for your child's conviction / conscience.

Holy Spirit, would You convict _____'s heart and turn him(her) from his(her) sins, cause _____ to turn toward You, God, so he(she) can be cleansed from his(her) sins. ~Amen (Acts 3:20 NLT)

NOTES:

March 15

Category: Integrity
Verse: 1 Chronicles 29:17-18
Focus: Pray for your child's heart.

Remind _____, dear Lord, that You examine his(her) heart and You will rejoice when You find integrity there. I pray that all that _____ does would be done with good motive. Help _____ want to obey You; may his(her) love for You never change. ~Amen (1 Chronicles 29:17-18 NLT)

NOTES:

March 16

Category: Blessing
Verse: James 3:13-16
Focus: Pray for character / godly wisdom for your child.

Heavenly Father, I pray that _____ would be wise and understand Your ways, God; bless him(her) with a life of steady goodness so that his(her) good deeds will pour forth. Don't let _____ become bitterly jealous, or have selfish ambition in his(her) heart, or brag about being wise. Give _____ wisdom that comes from heaven, may he(she) be peace loving, gentle at all times, and willing to yield to others. ~Amen (James 3:13-16 NLT)

NOTES:

March 17

Category: Temptation
Verse: Galatians 5:19-22
Focus: Prayer for the fruit of the Spirit for your child / asking for the Holy Spirit.

Gracious God, give _____ strength to not follow the desires of his(her) sinful nature, but rather may _____ let the Holy Spirit control his(her) life; for the Holy Spirit will produce in him(her) love, joy, peace, patience, kindness, goodness, faithfulness, gentleness, and self-control. ~Amen (Galatians 5:19-23 NLT)

NOTES:

March 18

Category: Character/Life Issues
Verse: Philippians 4:12-13
Focus: Prayer for Contentment for your child / satisfaction.

Dear God, help _____ to be satisfied, to know how to live on almost nothing or with everything. Help him(her) learn the secret of living in every situation, with plenty or little, is to do all things with the help of Christ who strengthens him(her). ~Amen (Philippians 4:12-13 NLT)

NOTES:

March 19

Category: Friendship
Verse: Philippians 1:4-7
Focus: Pray for your child's friendships.

Holy Father, give _____ a friend, a partner with whom he(she) can spread the Good News about Christ with. May they pray for each other, and have a special place in their hearts for each other. ~Amen (Philippians 1:4-7 NLT)

NOTES:

March 20

Category: Church
Verse: Exodus 20:8
Focus: Pray for Sabbath rest for your child / your child to observe the Sabbath.

Lord God, remind _____ to observe the Sabbath day by keeping it holy. May he(she) use six days for daily duties and rest on the seventh day, dedicating it to You, Lord. ~Amen
(Exodus 20:8 -10 NLT)

NOTES:

March 21

Category: Praise
Verse: Psalm 5:11
Focus: Pray a blessing over your child / for your child to have a joyful spirit.

Heavenly Father, may _____ take refuge in You, Lord, and rejoice. May he(she) sing joyful praises forever. Protect _____, Lord, so that he(she) will love Your name and be filled with joy. ~Amen (Psalm 5:11 NLT)

NOTES:

March 22

Category: Love God's Word
Verse: Psalm 19:7-9
Focus: Pray a blessing over your child / for your child to obey God's commandments.

Lord God, may _____ know the law of the Lord, may it revive his(her) soul. May _____ trust in the decrees of You Lord and gain wisdom. May _____ follow the commandments of the Lord, which are right and bring joy to the heart. May _____ obey the commands of the Lord which are clear and give insight to life. May _____ revere You, Lord, out of a pure heart. ~Amen (Psalm 19:7-9 NLT)

NOTES:

March 23

Category: Others
Verse: James 2:14-17
Focus: Pray for your child to have a giving spirit.

Gracious God, let _____ prove his(her) faith by his(her) actions: when he(she) sees those in need of food or clothing (or other things) may _____ live out his(her) faith and help them. ~Amen (James 2:14-17 NLT)

NOTES:

March 24

Category: Soul
Verse: Psalm 19:13-14
Focus: Pray for your child's heart.

Heavenly Father, may _____ offer You the sacrifice of a broken spirit; for a broken and repentant heart, O God, You will not despise. ~Amen (Psalm 51:17 NLT)

NOTES:

March 25

Category: Temptation
Verse: Psalm 19:13-14
Focus: Pray for your child's thoughts / integrity.

Lord, keep _____ from deliberate sins! Don't let sin control him(her). Instead, may the words of _____'s mouth and the thoughts of his(her) heart be pleasing to You, O Lord, the Rock, the Redeemer. ~Amen (Psalm 19:13-14 NLT)

NOTES:

March 26

Category: Soul / Faith
Verse: Numbers 32:23
Focus: Pray for your child's integrity and character.

Heavenly Father, help _____ to keep his(her) word and not sin against You, Lord. If _____ fails to keep his(her) word, may his(her) sin be found out. ~Amen (Numbers 32:23 NLT)

NOTES:

March 27

Category: Anxiety
Verse: Psalm 42:6
Focus: Pray for your child's soul.

O God, when _____'s soul is downcast, help him(her) remember You and put his(her) hope in You. ~Amen (Psalm 42:6 ESV)

NOTES:

March 28

Category: Temptation
Verse: 2 Timothy 2:22
Focus: Pray for your child to pursue faith.

Gracious God, cause _____ to run from anything that stimulates youthful lust. Instead, may he(she) follow anything that makes him(her) want to do right. May he(she) pursue faith and love and peace, and enjoy the companionship of those who call on the Lord with pure hearts. ~Amen (2 Timothy 2:22 NLT)

NOTES:

March 29

Category: Anxiety/Prodigal
Verse: Isaiah 40:11
Focus: Pray for your child to be cared for by God.

Lord, You have promised to feed Your flock like a shepherd. I pray that You will carry _____, Your lamb, in Your arms and hold him(her) close to Your heart. ~Amen (Isaiah 40:11 NLT)

NOTES:

March 30

Category: Family
Verse: Colossians 2:2
Focus: Pray for your child's sibling relationships.

Lord God, may _____ and his(her) siblings be knit together by strong ties of love. Give _____ full confidence and complete understanding of Your plan, and of Christ. ~Amen
(Colossians 2:2 NLT)

NOTES:

March 31

Category: Others
Verse: 1 Timothy 2:2
Focus: Pray for your child to be compassionate.

Gracious God, may _____ have a heart to pray for people and ask for You to show mercy to them. May he(she) pray for those in authority in his(her) life so that they can live in peace and quietness, in godliness and dignity. ~Amen
(1 Timothy 2:2 NLT)

NOTES:

April

Prayers from Scripture are powerful because the Word of God does not return void. You can be assured that you are praying God's will because you are praying God's words.

April 1

Category: Future
Verse: Job 1:10
Focus: Pray for your child's protection.

Lord, I pray that You would protect _____, his(her) home and his(her) property from all harm. Bless _____ and make him(her) prosperous in everything he(she) does. ~Amen (Job 1:10 NLT)

NOTES:

April 2

Category: Character
Verse: Philippians 1:6
Focus: Pray for God to be at work in your child.

Gracious God, You have begun a good work in _____, I pray that You will continue to do Your work in him(her) until it is finally finished. ~Amen (Philippians 1:6 NLT)

NOTES:

April 3

Category: Future
Verse: Genesis 29:20
Focus: Pray for your child's marriage partner.

Heavenly Father, I pray that _____ would be like Jacob: willing to wait for Your perfect timing in finding a spouse, and may that time pass quickly, as it did for Jacob. ~Amen (Genesis 29:20 NLT)

NOTES:

April 4

Category: Others Service
Verse: Ephesians 5:15-17
Focus: Pray for wise choices for your child.

Lord God, cause _____ to be careful how to live, may he(she) not be foolish but wise. Help _____ to make the most of every opportunity to do good to others, and to understand what Your will for him(her) is, Lord. ~Amen (Ephesians 5:15-15 NLT)

NOTES:

April 5

Category: Faith
Verse: 1 Timothy 1:5-6
Focus: Pray for your child to listen to God.

Heavenly Father, cause _____ to listen to Your instruction and be filled with love that comes from a pure heart, a clear conscience, and sincere faith. May _____ not turn away from these things and spend their time arguing and talking foolishness. ~Amen
(1 Timothy 1:5-6 NLT)

NOTES:

April 6

Category: Soul
Verse: 1 Timothy 2:4-5
Focus: Pray for your child to know God.

God, Your Word says that You want everyone to be saved and to understand the truth. May _____ know You as the only God and the One Mediator who can reconcile Himself with people. ~Amen (1 Timothy 2:4-5 NLT)

NOTES:

April 7

Category: Parent/Child Relationship
Verse: 1 Thessalonians 2:12
Focus: Pray for your child to live for God and be an encouraging parent. (1 Thessalonians 2:12)

Dear God, help me as a parent to encourage, comfort, and urge _____ to live a life worthy of God, who has called him(her) into his kingdom and glory. ~Amen (1 Thessalonians 2:12)

NOTES:

April 8

Category: Faith
Verse: 1 Thessalonians 2:13
Focus: Pray for your child to trust God's Word and live God's Word.

Heavenly Father, I pray that when _____ receives the Word of God, he(she) will accept it not as the word of men, but as it actually is, the Word of God, which is at work in those who believe. ~Amen (1 Thessalonians 2:13)

NOTES:

April 9

Category: Character
Verse: 1 Timothy 4:7
Focus: Pray for your child's spiritual fitness.

Dear God, may _____ not waste time arguing over godless ideas and old wives' tales. Help him(her) spend his(her) time and energy in training himself(herself) for spiritual fitness. ~Amen (1 Timothy 4:7 NLT)

NOTES:

April 10

Category: Friendship
Verse: 1 Timothy 4:12-13
Focus: Pray for your child to be a leader and a good example.

Heavenly Father, help _____ to be like Timothy and be a Christian example to those around him(her) in the way he(she) lives, in the way he(she) loves, by his(her) faith and purity. May _____ focus on reading the Scriptures, encouraging fellow believers and teaching them. ~Amen (1 Timothy 4:12-13 NLT)

NOTES:

April 11

Category: Life Issues
Verse: 1 Timothy 6:10
Focus: Pray for your child to manage money well.

Wise God, block _____ from craving money, for the love of money is at the root of all kinds of evil. Don't let him(her) wander from the faith and pierce him(herself) with many sorrows because he(she) seeks to have money. ~Amen (1 Timothy 6:10 NLT)

NOTES:

April 12

Category: Character
Verse: 1 Timothy 6:11
Focus: Pray for your child's resolve.

Heavenly Father, may _____ belong to You, God, and run from all things evil. May he(she) follow what is right and good, pursue a godly life, along with faith, love, perseverance, and gentleness. ~Amen (1 Timothy 6:11 NLT)

NOTES:

April 13

Category: Faith
Verse: 1 Timothy 6:20-21
Focus: Pray for your child to avoid gossip.

May _____ guard what You, dear God, have entrusted to him(her). Help _____ avoid godless, foolish discussion with those who oppose You with their so-called knowledge. Don't let _____ wander from the faith by following such foolishness. ~Amen (1 Timothy 6:20-21 NLT)

NOTES:

April 14

Category: Temptation
Verse: Galatians 5:1
Focus: Pray for your child to be a new creation.

Heavenly Father, remind _____ that Christ has really set him(her) free. Help _____ stay free, and not get tied up again in slavery to the law. ~Amen (Galatians 5:1 NLT)

NOTES:

April 15

Category: Character
Verse: Luke 2:52
Focus: Pray for wisdom and favor for your child.

Heavenly Father, may _____ grow as Jesus did, in wisdom and stature, and in favor with both God and men. ~Amen (Luke 2:52)

NOTES:

April 16

Category: Temptation / Prodigal
Verse: Romans 1:21-23
Focus: Pray for God's protection over your child's mind.

O God, I pray as _____ takes his(her) faith as his(her) own You will protect him(her); may he(she) never refuse to glorify You as God, or fail to show You gratitude; keep _____'s thinking from becoming nonsense, don't let _____'s mind become senseless or darkened; keep him(her) from becoming a fool by claiming to be wise; never let _____ exchange Your glory, immortal God, for any false image. ~Amen (Romans 1:21-23 HSCB)

NOTES:

April 17

Category: Temptation
Verse: James 1:22
Focus: Pray for your child to follow God.

Heavenly Father, I pray that _____ would realize that Your message is one to obey, not just to listen to. Show him(her) that by not obeying, he(she) is only fooling himself(herself). ~Amen (James 1:22 NLT)

NOTES:

April 18

Category: Blessing
Verse: Proverbs 3:5-6
Focus: Pray for your child to seek God.

May _____ trust in You, Lord, with all of his(her) heart, don't let him(her) depend on his(her) own understanding. May _____ seek Your will in all he(she) does, please direct his(her) paths. ~Amen (Proverbs 3:5-6 NLT)

NOTES:

April 19

Category: Faithful Living
Verse: Philippians 2:15-16
Focus: Pray for your child's values to shine.

Dear God, may _____ live a clean, innocent life as Your child, God, in this dark world full of crooked and perverse people. Let _____'s life shine brightly before others, and hold tightly to the Word of life. ~Amen (Philippians 2:15-16 NLT)

NOTES:

April 20

Category: Blessing
Verse: Proverbs 9:10-12
Focus: Pray for wisdom and blessings for your child.

Cause _____ to fear You, Lord, because that is the beginning of wisdom. Fill _____ with knowledge of the Holy One, that results in understanding. May wisdom multiply _____'s days and add years to his(her) life. ~Amen (Proverbs 9:10-12 NLT)

NOTES:

April 21

Category: Soul
Verse: John 3:16
Focus: Pray for your child's soul and life.

Thank You God, for loving _____ so much that You gave Your only Son, so that when _____ believes in You, he(she) will not perish but have eternal life. ~Amen (John 3:16 NLT)

NOTES:

April 22

Category: School
Verse: Psalm 37:40
Focus: Pray for your child's protection.

Lord, when _____ is attacked by bullies or other evils, I pray that You, Lord, would help him(her), rescue him(her) from the wicked. Be _____'s shelter. ~Amen (Psalm 37:40 NLT)

NOTES:

April 23

Category: Future
Verse: Ephesians 3:20-21
Focus: Pray for God to be at work in your child's life.

May Your mighty power be at work in _____. For You are able to accomplish infinitely more than he(she) would ever dare to ask or hope. ~Amen (Ephesians 3:20-21 NLT)

NOTES:

April 24

Category: Missions
Verse: Psalm 89:1
Focus: Pray for your child to praise God.

Heavenly Father, let _____ sing of Your love forever; let him(her) make known Your faithfulness through all generations. ~Amen (Psalm 89:1)

NOTES:

April 25

Category: Future
Verse: 1 Peter 3:7 & Ephesians 5:25
Focus: Pray for your child's future spouse.

Lord God, when _____ gets married, help him(her) to honor his(her) spouse and treat them with understanding as they live together. May _____ and his(her) spouse love each other with the same love Christ showed the church, willing to give him(herself) up for his(her) spouse. ~Amen (1 Peter 3:7 & Ephesians 5:25 NLT)

NOTES:

April 26

Category: Faithful Living
Verse: 1 Corinthians 2:9 & Isaiah 64:4
Focus: Pray for God's work in your child's life.

Thank You, God, for the Scriptures, in them You tell us: No eye has seen, no ear has heard, and no mind has imagined what You have prepared for _____ because You love him(her). Help _____ be willing to wait for You to work on his(her) behalf. ~Amen (1 Corinthians 2:9 & Isaiah 64:4 NLT)

NOTES:

April 27

Category: School
Verse: Galatians 6:9
Focus: Pray for your child's teachers and coaches.

Heavenly Father, let _____'s teacher and coaches not get tired of doing what is good. Help them not become discouraged and give up, but help them see that they will reap a harvest of blessing at the appropriate time. And, help _____ not to give up praying for their teachers and coaches. ~Amen (Galatians 6:9 NLT)

NOTES:

April 28

Category: Soul
Verse: Psalm 71:5
Focus: Pray for your child's salvation.

May You, O Sovereign Lord, be _____'s hope; may his(her) confidence be in You from childhood. ~Amen (Psalm 71:5)

NOTES:

April 29

Category: Character
Verse: Philippians 2:14
Focus: Pray for your child's arguing.

Gracious God, In everything _____ does, may he(she) stay away from complaining and arguing. ~Amen. (Philippians 2:14 NLT)

NOTES:

April 30

Category: Parent/Child Relationship
Verse: Ephesians 6:1-3
Focus: Pray for your child to honor parents.

Dear Lord, cause _____ to obey us as parents, because he(she) belongs to You, Lord, for this is the right thing to do. May _____ honor his(her) father and mother, so that he(she) will live a long life, full of blessing. ~Amen (Ephesians 6:1-3 NLT)

NOTES:

May

Entrusting your child to God through prayer brings comfort and peace. Have confidence that God hears you and loves you.

May 1

Category: Friendship
Verse: Proverbs 12:26 & 1 Corinthians 15:33
Focus: Pray for your child's friendships.

Dear God, I pray that _____ would give good advice to his(her) friends. Remind _____ that bad company corrupts good morals. ~Amen (Proverbs 12:26 & 1 Corinthians 15:33 NLT)

NOTES:

May 2

Category: Protection
Verse: Psalm 17:8-9
Focus: Pray for your child's protection.

Heavenly Father, I pray that You would guard _____ as the apple of Your eye; hide him(her) in the shadow of Your wings. Protect _____ from wicked people who might attack him(her). ~Amen (Psalm 17:8-9 NLT)

NOTES:

May 3

Category: Faith
Verse: 2 Corinthians 10:4-5
Focus: Pray for boldness in spiritual warfare for your child.

Lord God, remind _____ to use Your mighty weapons, God, not mere worldly weapons, to knock down the Devil's strongholds. May _____ use these weapons to break down every proud argument that keeps people from knowing You, God. With these weapons help _____ conquer others rebellious ideas and help he(she) teach others to obey Christ. ~Amen (2 Corinthians 10:4-5 NLT)

NOTES:

May 4

Category: Character
Verse: Proverbs 3:7-8
Focus: Pray for your child's humbleness.

Heavenly Father, keep _____ from being impressed with his(her) own wisdom. Instead, may _____ fear You, Lord, and turn his(her) back on evil so that he(she) will gain renewed health and vitality. ~Amen (Proverbs 3:7-8 NLT)

NOTES:

May 5

Category: Character
Verse: Psalm 141:3-4
Focus: Pray for self-control for your child and your child's words.

Gracious God, at the right times, Lord, would You take control of what _____ says, and keep his(her) lips sealed. May _____ look to You for help, O Sovereign Lord, and be _____'s refuge. ~Amen (Psalm 141:3,8 NLT)

NOTES:

May 6

Category: Integrity
Verse: Proverbs 1:3
Focus: Pray for your child to be disciplined.

Dear God, I pray that _____ would live a disciplined and prudent life, help him(her) do what is right and just and fair. ~Amen (Proverbs 1:3 NIV)

NOTES:

May 7

Category: Friend
Verse: Psalm 101:6
Focus: Pray for your child's friendships.

Heavenly Father, give _____ faithful people to be his(her) companions. ~Amen (Psalm 101:6 NLT)

NOTES:

May 8

Category: Character
Verse: 2 Corinthians 9:11
Focus: Pray for your child to be generous.

Lord, please enrich _____ in every way so that he(she) can always be generous. Because of his(her) generous spirit may people thank You, God. ~ Amen (2 Corinthians 9:11)

NOTES:

May 9

Category: Character
Verse: 2 Peter 1:2-3
Focus: Pray for your child to have grace and peace.

God, would You give _____ more and more grace and peace as he(she) grows in knowledge of You. Give _____ everything he(she) needs for living a godly life. ~Amen (2 Peter 1:2-3)

NOTES:

May 10

Category: Love God's Word
Verse: John 14:21
Focus: Pray for your child's faith.

Heavenly Father, cause _____ to know Your commands and obey them out of his(her) love for You. Thank You for loving _____, Father. ~Amen (John 14:21 NLT)

NOTES:

May 11

Category: Future Work Ethic
Verse: Proverbs 22:29
Focus: Pray for your child's skills and talents.

Gracious God, teach _____ to be a person skilled in their work, so that he(she) may serve before kings. ~Amen (Proverbs 22:29 NLT)

NOTES:

May 12

Category: Missions
Verse: Matthew 4:19
Focus: Pray for your child's faith journey/to follow Jesus.

Holy Father, give _____ the desire to follow after You, Jesus, and make _____ a fisher of people. ~Amen (Matthew 4:19 NLT)

NOTES:

May 13

Category: Faithful Living
Verse: Psalm 16:7, 11
Focus: Pray for your child to seek God's counsel.

Heavenly Father, may _____ praise You, Lord, as You counsel him(her). Because You are at _____'s right hand he(she) will not be shaken. Let _____ experience the joys of life and the exquisite pleasures of Your own eternal presence. ~ Amen
(Psalm 16:7, 11 NLT)

NOTES:

May 14

Category: Mind and Body
Verse: Ephesians 2:10
Focus: Pray for your child's ministry.

Dear God, remind _____ that he(she) is Your workmanship, created in Christ Jesus to do good works, works which You have prepared in advance for _____ to do. ~Amen
(Ephesians 2:10 NLT)

NOTES:

May 15

Category: Anger
Verse: Psalm 103:8
Focus: Pray for your child to be compassionate.

Dear Lord, may _____ be like You--compassionate and gracious, may _____ be slow to anger and abounding in love. ~Amen
(Psalm 103:8 NLT)

NOTES:

May 16

Category: Friend
Verse: Titus 2:1-2
Focus: Pray for a mentor and faithful friends for your child.

Dear God, surround _____ with people whose lives reflect
wholesome teaching, with people who exercise self-control,
are worthy of respect, and those that live wisely. Let him(her)
witness those that have a sound faith and are filled with love and
patience. ~Amen (Titus 2:1-2 NLT)

NOTES:

May 17

Category: Temptation
Verse: Proverbs 2:7-8
Focus: Pray for God's protection over your child.

Lord, I pray that You would be a shield to _____, help him(her)
be upright and give him(her) victory. Guard _____'s course and
protect his(her) way. ~Amen (Proverbs 2:7-8 NLT)

NOTES:

May 18

Category: Integrity
Verse: Titus 2:6-8
Focus: Pray for your child to be free from temptation and sin.

Gracious God, may _____, as a young person, be self-controlled. Help _____ be an example to others by doing what is good; help _____ have integrity and soundness of speech. ~Amen (Titus 2:6-8 NLT)

NOTES:

May 19

Category: Soul
Verse: Matthew 5:3
Focus: Pray for your child to know God.

God, would You bless _____ and help him(her) see his(her) need for You, for You promised that the Kingdom of Heaven will be given to him(her). ~Amen (Matthew 5:3 NLT)

NOTES:

May 20

Category: Anxiety
Verse: Matthew 5:4
Focus: Pray the Beatitudes for your child.

God, would You bless _____ when he(she) mourns, for You promise to comfort him(her). ~Amen (Matthew 5:4 NLT)

NOTES:

May 21

Category: Faithful Living
Verse: Matthew 5:6
Focus: Pray for your child to hunger and thirst for righteousness.

Dear God, would You bless _____ and cause him(her) to hunger and thirst for righteousness, for You have promised to fill those who hunger for You. ~Amen (Matthew 5:6)

NOTES:

May 22

Category: Faithful Living
Verse: Matthew 5:7
Focus: Pray for your child to have a merciful heart.

Dear Lord, I pray that You would bless _____ with a merciful spirit, a merciful heart, for You have promised to show him(her) mercy. ~Amen (Matthew 5:7)

NOTES:

May 23

Category: Heart
Verse: Matthew 5:8
Focus: Pray for your child to have a pure heart.

Dear God, bless _____ and give him(her) a pure heart; for those pure in heart will see You. ~Amen (Matthew 5:8)

NOTES:

May 24

Category: Heart
Verse: Matthew 5:9
Focus: Pray for your child to be a peacemaker.

Dear Lord, bless _____ with the heart of a peacemaker, for the peacemakers will be called sons of God. ~Amen (Matthew 5:9)

NOTES:

May 25

Category: Service
Verse: Matthew 5:10
Focus: Pray God's strength for your child in times of adversity.

Gracious God, bless _____ when he(she) is persecuted because of righteousness, those who persecuted will be given the kingdom of heaven. ~Amen (Matthew 5:10)

NOTES:

May 26

Category: Missions
Verse: Matthew 5:11-12
Focus: Pray for your child's inner strength.

Heavenly Father, bless _____ when he(she) is insulted or persecuted, or when others falsely say all kinds of evil against him(her) because of Christ. May _____ rejoice and be glad because his(her) reward is in heaven. ~Amen
(Matthew 5:11-12)

NOTES:

May 27

Category: Missions
Verse: Matthew 5:13-14
Focus: Pray for your child to be a light in the world.

God, bless _____ help him(her) be the salt of the earth, a light to the world, a city on a hill that cannot be hidden. ~Amen
(Matthew 5:13-14)

NOTES:

May 28

Category: Mind and Body
Verse: Matthew 5:34, 37
Focus: Pray for your child's words.

Dear Lord, help _____ to not swear at all. Let his(her) "Yes" simply be "Yes" and his(her) "No" simply be "No." ~Amen (Matthew 5:34, 37)

NOTES:

May 29

Category: Friendship
Verse: Matthew 5:41
Focus: Pray for your child to be generous.

Gracious God, grow _____ into the kind of person who, if asked to go a mile for someone, will go two miles. ~Amen (Matthew 5:41)

NOTES:

May 30

Category: Friendship
Verse: Matthew 5:44
Focus: Pray for your child to love others.

Heavenly Father, may _____ be the kind of person who loves his(her) enemies and prays for those who persecute him(her), please show that he(she) is a son(daughter) of heaven. ~Amen (Matthew 5:44)

NOTES:

May 31

Category: Character
Verse: 2 Corinthians 15:16
Focus: Pray for your child to be a blessing.

Heavenly Father, may _____'s life be a fragrance presented by Christ to God; may he(she) be a life-giving perfume to those around him(her). ~Amen (2 Corinthians 15-16 NLT)

NOTES:

June

Praying Scripture: One moment, one prayer, one life changed by the power of God's Word.

June 1

Category: Mind and Body
Verse: 1 Timothy 2:9
Focus: Pray for your child's clothing choices.

Glorious God, may _____ be modest in his(her) appearance. Remind him(her) to wear decent and appropriate clothing so he(she) won't draw attention to himself(herself) or cause others to stumble into sin when they look at him(her). ~Amen (1 Timothy 2:9 NLT)

NOTES:

June 2

Category: Blessing
Verse: Psalm 1:1-2
Focus: Pray for your child to delight in God.

Gracious God, may _____ know the joys of those who do not
follow the advice of the wicked, or stand around
with sinners, or join in with scoffers. Instead, may
_____ delight in doing everything You, want, O Lord; day and
night help _____ think about Your law. ~Amen (Psalm 1:1-2 NLT)

NOTES:

June 3

Category: Parent/Child Relationship
Verse: Malachi 4:6
Focus: Pray for God to turn your child's heart.

Lord God, turn my heart, Lord, towards _____; and turn _____'s
heart toward us, their parents. ~Amen (Malachi 4:6 NLT)

NOTES:

June 4

Category: Missions
Verse: Romans 12:13
Focus: Pray for your child to help others.

Heavenly Father, I pray that _____ would share with God's people who are in need, may he(she) be always ready to help them. And may _____ always be eager to practice hospitality. ~Amen (Romans 12:13)

NOTES:

June 5

Category: Soul
Verse: Romans 10:9
Focus: Pray for your child to become a follower of Christ.

Gracious God, I pray that _____ would confess with his(her) mouth that Jesus is Lord, and believe in his(her) heart that You raised Jesus from the dead, so that he(she) will be saved. ~Amen (Romans 10:9 NLT)

NOTES:

June 6

Category: Character
Verse: Proverbs 31:25, 30
Focus: Pray for your child's strength.

Lord God, may _____ be clothed with strength and dignity, help him(her) laugh with no fear of the future. Remind _____ that charm is deceptive, beauty does not last, but the one who fears the Lord will be greatly praised. ~Amen (Proverbs 31:25, 30 NLT)

NOTES:

June 7

Category: Parent/Child Relationship
Verse: Proverbs 1:8-9
Focus: Pray for you child to respect their parents.

Gracious God, I pray that _____ would listen to what his(her) father teaches him(her). May _____ not neglect his(her) mother's teaching. Let _____ see that what he(she) learns from a parent will crown him(her) with grace and clothe him(her) with honor. ~Amen (Proverbs 1:8-9 NLT)

NOTES:

June 8

Category: Soul
Verse: Acts 26:18
Focus: Pray for your child's faith.

Gracious God, I pray that you would open _____'s eyes so he(she) can see the difference between dark and light; may _____ choose light. Help _____ see the difference between Satan and God, and choose God. May he(she) clearly see Your offer of forgiveness of sins, and choose a place in the family, in the company of those who begin real living by believing in You, Christ. ~Amen (Acts 26:18 MSG)

NOTES:

June 9

Category: Praise
Verse: Psalm 122:1
Focus: Pray for your child to enjoy worshipping God.

Heavenly Father, may _____ be like David, who is glad with those that say, "Let us go to the house of the Lord." May he(she) love to praise You. ~Amen (Psalm 122:1 NLT)

NOTES:

June 10

Category: Love God's Word
Verse: Acts 17:11
Focus: Pray for your child to love God's Word.

Gracious God, may _____ be like a Berean and listen eagerly to the messages in church. Prompt _____ to search the Scriptures day after day to check up on the pastor's teaching, and see if they are teaching the truth. ~Amen (Acts 17:11 NLT)

NOTES:

June 11

Category: Future
Verse: Matthew 26:41
Focus: Pray for your child's dating life.

Lord God, when _____ is yearning for a dating relationship, help him(her) to stay alert and pray, so that temptation will not overpower him(her). Strengthen _____'s spirit when his(her) body is weak. ~Amen (Matthew 26:41 NLT)

NOTES:

June 12

Category: Character
Verse: Luke 22:31-32
Focus: Pray for your child's faith.

Heavenly Father, when Satan asks to sift _____ like wheat, I pray, as You do Jesus, that his(her) faith will not fail him(her); please strengthen and build up _____. ~Amen (Luke 22:31-32 NLT)

NOTES:

June 13

Category: Prodigal
Verse: Psalm 125:2
Focus: Pray for God's protection over your child.

Lord God, just as the mountains surround and protect Jerusalem, Lord, I pray that You would surround and protect _____, both now and forevermore. ~Amen (Psalm 125:2 NLT)

NOTES:

June 14

Category: Work Ethic
Verse: 1 Corinthians 9:24-25
Focus: Pray for your child's goals.

Holy Father, remind _____ of the value of strict training. Help him(her) to run the race in such a way as to be the one who gets the prize. ~Amen (1 Corinthians 9:24-25 NLT)

NOTES:

June 15

Category: School
Verse: Proverbs 16:24
Focus: Pray for your child to use kind words in school.

Lord God, may _____ use kind words, words that are like honey-- sweet to the soul and healthy for the body. ~Amen (Proverbs 16:24 NLT)

NOTES:

June 16

Category: Temptation
Verse: Romans 12:1 & 1 Corinthians 6:18-20
Focus: Pray for your child's body to be God's temple.

Dear Lord, help _____ to give his(her) body to You, God. May
he(she) be a living and holy sacrifice. Help _____ to run away
from sexual sin, remembering that his(her) body is a temple of the
Holy Spirit. ~Amen (Romans 12:1 & 1 Corinthians 6:18-20 NLT)

NOTES:

June 17

Category: Others
Verse: 1 Peter 2:17
Focus: Pray for your child to be respectful.

Gracious God, may _____ have respect for everyone, and love
his(her) Christian brothers and sisters. May _____ fear God, and
respect those in authority over him(her) (including teachers and
coaches). ~Amen (1 Peter 2:17 NLT)

NOTES:

June 18

Category: Soul
Verse: Philippians 2:13
Focus: Pray for God's work in your child's life.

Heavenly Father, remind _____, God, that You are working in him(her), and give _____ the desire and power to do what pleases You. ~Amen (Philippians 2:13 NLT)

NOTES:

June 19

Category: Life Issues
Verse: Philippians 4:19 & 1 Chronicles 29:14
Focus: Pray for your child to be confidence in God's provision.

Dear Lord, remind _____ that everything he(she) has comes from You, and that You, the God who cares for _____, will supply all of his(her) needs from Your glorious riches, which have been given to us in Christ. ~Amen
(1 Chronicles 29:14 & Philippians 4:19 NLT)

NOTES:

June 20

Category: Future
Verse: Isaiah 48:17
Focus: Pray for God's leading in your child's life.

Lord God, I pray that You would be _____'s Lord and God, be the one who teaches him(her) what is good; please lead _____ on the only path he(she) should follow. ~Amen (Isaiah 48:17 NLT)

NOTES:

June 21

Category: Soul
Verse: 1 John 1:9 & 2 Corinthians 5:17
Focus: Pray for your child's heart.

Heavenly Father, may _____ confess his(her) sins to You, knowing You are faithful and just to forgive him(her) of sin and cleanse him(her) from all wickedness. Remind _____ that he(she) belongs to You and is a new person...the old life is gone, a new life has begun! ~Amen (1 John 1:9 & 2 Corinthians 5:17 NLT)

NOTES:

June 22

Category: Heart
Verse: Ezekiel 11:19-20
Focus: Pray for your child's spirit.

Lord, I pray that You would give _____ singleness of heart and a put a new spirit within him(her). May You take away _____'s stony, stubborn heart and give him(her) a tender, responsive heart; help him(her) obey Your decrees and regulations and be _____'s God. ~Amen (Ezekiel 11:19-20 NLT)

NOTES:

June 23

Category: Character
Verse: 2 Timothy 3:16
Focus: Pray for your child to do to God's Word.

Heavenly Father, would You show _____ that all Scripture is inspired by You, God, and is useful to teach what is true. May Your Word make _____ realize what is wrong in his(her) life, may it correct his(her) when he(she) is wrong and may it teach him(her) to do what is right. ~Amen (2 Timothy 3:16 NLT)

NOTES:

June 24

Category: Relationship
Verse: 1 Peter 4:10-11
Focus: Pray for your child to serve others.

God, You have given each of us a gift from Your great variety of spiritual gifts; cause _____ to use his(her) gifts well, to serve others. May _____ serve others with strength and energy that You supply God, and bring You glory. ~Amen (1 Peter 4:10-11 NLT)

NOTES:

June 25

Category: Faithful Living
Verse: Psalm 130
Focus: Pray for your child to come to God and learn to rely on Him.

Lord, if You kept a record of our sins, who, O Lord, could ever survive? Remind _____ that You offer forgiveness, help him(her) learn to fear You and learn to count on You, Lord. May _____ put his(her) hope in Your Word. ~Amen (Psalm 130:3-5 NLT)

NOTES:

June 26

Category: Character/Temptation
Verse: Proverbs 4:5-7
Focus: Pray for wisdom for your child.

Lord God, may _____ pursue wisdom, and not turn his(her)
back on it. May _____ develop good judgment and not forget
Your words God. May _____ prize wisdom and realize it's value.
~Amen (Proverbs 4:5-7 NLT)

NOTES:

June 27

Category: Friendship
Verse: 2 Corinthians 1:4
Focus: Pray for your child to be comforted by God.

Heavenly Father, I ask that You would comfort _____ in all of
his(her) troubles, so that he(she) can comfort others when they
are troubled, with the same comfort You have given him(her).
~Amen (2 Corinthians 1:4 NLT)

NOTES:

June 28

Category: Faithful Living
Verse: Psalm 37:1-7
Focus: Pray a blessing over your child.

May _____ trust in You, Lord and do good. May _____ delight himself(herself) in You, May _____ commit his(her) ways to You, Lord, and trust in You. May _____ be still and know that You are the Lord, and that You wait patiently for him(her). Lord, would You give _____ the desires of his(her) heart. ~Amen (Psalm 37:1-7)

NOTES:

June 29

Category: Blessing
Verse: Psalm 139:5, 10
Focus: Pray God's blessing for your child.

Gracious God, I ask that You would go before _____. Please place Your hand of blessing on his(her) head. ~Amen (Psalm 139:5, 10 NLT)

NOTES:

June 30

Category: Friendship
Verse: Ecclesiastes 4:9, 12
Focus: Pray for your child's friendships.

Heavenly Father, would You bless _____ with friends who will reach out and help when he(she) falls; friends who can stand back to back and together conquer when attacked. ~Amen (Ecclesiastes 4: 9, 12 NLT)

NOTES:

July

Your prayers will guide and your child in the ways of the Lord. The fervent prayers of the righteous accomplish much.

July 1

Category: Blessing
Verse: Proverbs 6:20-23
Focus: Pray for your child to listen to wise words.

Dear God, may _____ obey his(her) father's commands, and not neglect his(her) mother's instruction. May _____ keep Your Words always in his(her) heart, and tie them around his(her) neck. When he(she) walks, let Your counsel guide him(her); when he(she) sleeps, may Your Words protect him(her); when he(she) wakes up, may Your Words advise him(her). May _____ see our commands as a lamp, our instruction as a light, and our corrective discipline as a way to life. ~Amen (Proverbs 6:20-23 NLT)

NOTES:

July 2

Category: Family
Verse: 2 Timothy 2:24-26
Focus: Pray for your child to serve others.

Heavenly Father, do not permit _____ to be quarrelsome; instead, cause him(her) to be gentle, patient, and humble, especially when his(her) siblings are in the wrong...because then they will be more likely, with God's help, to turn away from their wrong ideas and believe what is true. ~Amen (2 Timothy 2:24-26)

NOTES:

July 3

Category: Life Issues
Verse: Hebrews 13:5 & Philippians 4:12
Focus: Pray for your child's finances.

Father, keep _____'s life free from the love of money and let him(her) be content with that he(she) has, knowing that You, O Lord, will never leave him(her) or forsake him(her). Let _____ be like Paul, who knew how to be content in any and every situation, whether well fed or hungry, whether living in plenty or in want. ~Amen (Hebrews 13:5; Philippians 4:12)

NOTES:

July 4

Category: Parent/Child Relationship
Verse: Proverbs 22:6
Focus: Pray about training your child in the ways of the Lord.

Heavenly Father, help us to train _____ in the way that he(she) should go, so that when he(she) is old he(she) will not turn from it. ~Amen (Proverbs 22:6)

NOTES:

July 5

Category: Mind and Body
Verse: Ephesians 3:17-19
Focus: Pray for your child to be rooted in God.

Heavenly Father, I pray that _____'s identity will be firmly rooted and established in Christ's love, and that _____ may have power, together with all the saints, to grasp how wide and long and high and deep is the love of Christ, and to know this love that surpasses knowledge--that he(she) may be filled to the measure of all the fullness of God. ~Amen (Ephesians 3:17-19)

NOTES:

July 6

Category: Thanks
Verse: Colossians 2:6-7
Focus: Pray for your child to be thankful.

Heavenly Father, I pray that _____ would continue to live in Christ, rooted and built up in Him, strengthened in faith as he(she) was taught, and overflowing with thankfulness. ~Amen (Colossians 2:6-7)

NOTES:

July 7

Category: Future
Verse: Psalm 119:105
Focus: Pray for God's Word in your child's life.

Dear Lord, I pray that Your Word would be a lamp to _____'s feet and a light for his(her) path. ~Amen (Psalm 119:105 ESV)

NOTES:

July 8

Category: Faith/Missions
Verse: 1 Peter 3:15
Focus: Pray for your child to share their faith.

Heavenly Father, I pray that _____ would always be prepared to give an answer to everyone who asks him(her) to give the reason for the hope he(she) has, and cause _____ to speak with gentleness and with respect. ~Amen (1 Peter 3:15)

NOTES:

July 9

Category: Service
Verse: Ephesians 6:7-8
Focus: Pray for your child to have a servant's heart.

Gracious Father, I pray that You would motivate _____ to serve wholeheartedly, as if he(she) was serving You, not people; remind _____ that You will reward everyone for whatever good they do. ~Amen (Ephesians 6:7-8)

NOTES:

July 10

Category: Others
Verse: 2 John 3:17-18
Focus: Pray for your child to love others.

Heavenly Father, Your Word says that if anyone has material possessions and sees their brother in need but has no pity on them, how can the love of God be in him(her)? I pray that You would cause _____ to love others not merely with words, but let him(her) love others in actions and in truth. ~Amen (1 John 3:17-18)

NOTES:

July 11

Category: Temptation
Verse: James 4:7-8
Focus: Pray for your child to be strong during temptation.

Heavenly Father, I pray that You help _____ submit to You, O God, and to resist the devil. Make the devil flee from _____ as he(she) draws near to You. ~Amen (James 4:7-8)

NOTES:

July 12

Category: Friendship
Verse: Ephesians 4:29
Focus: Pray for your child to be an encourager.

Gracious Father, do not let any unwholesome talk come out of
_____'s mouth, but only what is helpful for building others up
according to their needs, that it may benefit those who listen.
~Amen (Ephesians 4:29)

NOTES:

July 13

Category: Family
Verse: 1 Peter 3:8-9a
Focus: Pray for your child and their sibling relationships.

Lord God, I pray that You would help _____ live in harmony with
his(her) siblings, help _____ be sympathetic, compassionate, and
humble. Don't let _____ and his(her) sibling(s) repay evil with evil
or insult with insult, but with blessing. ~Amen (1 Peter 3:8-9a)

NOTES:

July 14

Category: Blessing
Verse: 2 Thessalonians 1:11-12
Focus: Pray a blessing for your child.

Heavenly Father, fulfill every good purpose in _____'s life and every act prompted by his(her) faith, I pray this so that the name of our Lord Jesus Christ may be glorified in _____'s life. ~Amen (2 Thessalonians 1:11-12)

NOTES:

July 15

Category: Blessing
Verse: Psalm 3:3
Focus: Pray for God's blessings in your child's life.

Gracious Father, be a shield, O Lord, around _____; bestow glory on _____ and lift up his(her) head. ~Amen (Psalm 3:3)

NOTES:

July 16

Category: Life Issues
Verse: Luke 16:10-13
Focus: Pray for your child's financial decisions.

Heavenly Father, I pray that _____ would be trustworthy in how he(she) handles money and wealth, and that _____ would be single minded in his(her) devotion to You, recognizing that he(she) cannot serve both God and money. ~Amen (Luke 16:10-13)

NOTES:

July 17

Category: Character
Verse: 1 Corinthians 13:5
Focus: Pray for your child to love others.

Dear Lord, may _____'s life be marked by love, love that is not rude or self-seeking; may _____ not easily be angered or keep any record of wrongs. ~Amen (1 Corinthians 13:5)

NOTES:

July 18

Category: Faithful Living
Verse: Titus 3:4-5
Focus: Pray for your child's spiritual life.

God, You are the Savior, I pray that You would show _____ Your kindness and Your love. Save _____, not because of anything he(she) has done but because of Your mercy. Wash away _____'s sins and give him(her) new life through the Holy Spirit. ~Amen (Titus 3:4-5 NLT)

NOTES:

July 19

Category: Character
Verse: Psalm 13:5-6
Focus: Pray for your child's heart transformation.

Gracious God, help _____ to trust in Your unfailing love, cause _____'s heart to rejoice in Your salvation. May _____ sing to You, Lord, remind _____ of the ways You have been good to him(her). ~Amen (Psalm 13:5-6)

NOTES:

July 20

Category: Thanks
Verse: 1 Thessalonians 5:16-18
Focus: Pray for your child to be joyful.

Heavenly Father, let _____ always be joyful. Let _____ keep on praying. No matter what happens, let _____ always be thankful, for this is God's will for him(her), and for those who belong to Christ Jesus. ~Amen (1 Thessalonians 5:16-18 NLT)

NOTES:

July 21

Category: Future
Verse: Nehemiah 1:11
Focus: Pray for your child's success.

Lord, I pray that Your ear would be attentive to _____, may he(she) be a servant who delights in revering Your name; Give _____ success today by granting him(her) favor. ~Amen (Nehemiah 1:11)

NOTES:

July 22

Category: Praise
Verse: 1 Samuel 12:24
Focus: Pray for your child to revere God.

Gracious God, may _____ be sure to fear You, Lord, and sincerely worship You. Bring to his(her) mind all the wonderful things You have done for him(her). ~Amen (1 Samuel 12:24 NLT)

NOTES:

July 23

Category: Family
Verse: Romans 12:10
Focus: Pray for the relationship between your kids.

Lord, I pray that _____ and his(her) siblings would love each other with genuine affection, and take delight in honoring each other. ~Amen (Romans 12:10 NLT)

NOTES:

July 24

Category: Prodigal
Verse: Psalm 55:16-18
Focus: Pray for your child when in crisis or distress.

Gracious God, remind _____ to call on You, God, for You will rescue him(her). Be it morning, noon, or night when _____ is in distress, You, O Lord, hear his(her) voice. Rescue _____ and keep him(her) safe. ~Amen (Psalm 55:16-18 NLT)

NOTES:

July 25

Category: Prodigal
Verse: John 10:4-5
Focus: Pray for your child to walk in God's truth.

Lord God, I pray that _____ would know Your voice, as his(her) shepherd; may he(she) never follow a stranger, in fact may he(she) run away when the don't recognize the stranger's voice. ~Amen (John 10:4-5)

NOTES:

July 26

Category: School
Verse: Titus 3:1-2
Focus: Pray for our child's character.

Heavenly Father, remind _____ to be subject to the rulers and authorities in his(her) life, to be obedient, to be ready to do whatever is good, and to slander no one (even if _____ doesn't agree with a decision made by a parent/teacher/coach). Prompt _____ to be peaceable and considerate and to show true humility toward everyone. ~Amen (Titus 3:1-2)

NOTES:

July 27

Category: Others
Verse: Matthew 25:35-40
Focus: Pray for your child to have compassion.

Lord God, fill _____ with compassion: when he(she) sees someone who is hungry, may he(she) feed them or give them drink, may _____ be inviting, give clothing, care for the sick, visit those in prison...meet the needs of others and by doing so show the love of Christ. ~Amen (Matthew 25:35-40 NLT)

NOTES:

July 28

Category: Love God's Word
Verse: Psalm 27:8-9
Focus: Pray for your child's heart.

Lord, when _____'s heart hears You say, "Come and talk to me," may his(her) heart respond, "Lord, I am coming." ~Amen (Psalm 27:89 NLT)

NOTES:

July 29

Category: Missions
Verse: Philemon 1:6
Focus: Pray that your child with share their faith.

Heavenly Father, I pray that _____ will be active in sharing his(her) faith. ~Amen (Philemon 1:6)

NOTES:

July 30

Category: Character
Verse: Proverbs 4:11
Focus: Pray for your child's future.

Gracious God, I pray that You will guide _____ in the way of wisdom and lead _____ along straight paths. ~Amen (Proverbs 4:11)

NOTES:

July 31

Category: Work Ethic
Verse: Proverbs 6:9-11
Focus: Pray for your child's work ethic.

O God, some days I wonder how long _____ will laze around doing nothing, how long until he(she) gets out of bed. I pray that You show _____ that a nap here, a nap there, a day off here, a day off there can lead to a dirt-poor life, with poverty as his(her) permanent houseguest. ~Amen (Proverbs 6:9-11 MSG)

NOTES:

August

Prayer changes things. Turn your child over to God in prayer.

August 1

Category: Missions
Verse: Daniel 5:21
Focus: Pray for your child's school.

Heavenly Father, help _____ learn that You, the Most High God who rules over the kingdoms of the world and appoints anyone He desires to rule over them, places authorities in his(her) life for Your purposes. ~Amen (Daniel 5:21 NLT)

NOTES:

August 2

Category: School
Verse: Matthew 6:8 & Romans 8:28
Focus: Pray for your child's school schedule.

Heavenly Father, You know our needs before we ask You, Lord, and You promise to work in all things for the good of those who love You. Handpick each one of _____'s teachers and surround him(her) with classmates of Your choosing. ~Amen
(Matthew 6:8 & Romans 8:28)

NOTES:

August 3

Category: School
Verse: Isaiah 65:23b
Focus: Pray for the students at your child's school.

Lord, I pray that the Christians at _____ school will be a people blessed by You, they and their descendants. ~Amen
(Isaiah 65:23b)

NOTES:

August 4

Category: Family
Verse: Romans 14:19
Focus: Pray that your child will get along with family members.

Dear God, I pray that my children would use all his(her) energy in getting along with each other; help them choose encouraging words and not drag each other down by finding fault. ~Amen (Romans 14:19 MSG)

NOTES:

August 5

Category: Faithful Living
Verse: Psalm 25:14-15
Focus: Pray for your child to focus on God and be a friend of God.

Lord, You promise to be a friend to those who fear You. Be _____'s friend and teach him(her) about Your covenant. Help _____ keep his(her) eyes on You, rescue him(her) from the traps of the enemy. ~Amen (Psalm 25:14-15)

NOTES:

August 6

Category: Soul
Verse: Psalm 84:10
Focus: Pray for your child's loyalty.

Heavenly Father, may _____ choose to be a doorkeeper to Your house, O Lord, than live the good life in the homes of the wicked. ~Amen (Psalm 84:10 NLT)

NOTES:

August 7

Category: Parent/Child Relationship
Verse: Colossians 3:15
Focus: Pray for your child to have a peaceful heart.

Lord, would You help _____ let the peace that comes from Christ rule in his(her) heart. You have called us, may _____ live in peace and always be thankful. ~Amen (Colossians 3:15 NLT)

NOTES:

August 8

Category: Temptation
Verse: 1 Samuel 30:6b
Focus: Pray for your child's school year.

Gracious God, may _____ be like David, and find his(her) strength in You, Lord God. ~Amen (1 Samuel 30:6b)

NOTES:

August 9

Category: Praise
Verse: 1 Chronicles 16:8-11
Focus: Pray a blessing over your child's school year.

Heavenly Father, may _____ give thanks to You, God, and call on Your name. May he(she) sing to You and tell of all Your wonderful acts. May _____ glory in Your holy name; as he(she) seeks You, let him(her) rejoice. May _____ look to You, Lord and to Your strength, may _____ seek Your face always. ~Amen (1 Chronicles 16:8-11)

NOTES:

August 10

Category: Temptation
Verse: 2 Timothy 2:25-26
Focus: Pray for your child's mentors.

Heavenly Father, put people in _____'s life who will gently instruct him(her); and grant _____ repentance and lead him(her) to a knowledge of the Truth. Cause _____ to come to his(her) senses and escape the trap of the devil, who has taken him(her) captive to do his will. ~Amen (2 Timothy 2:25-26)

NOTES:

August 11

Category: Love God's Word
Verse: Psalm 1:1-3
Focus: Pray for your child to enjoy God's Word.

Gracious God, I pray that _____ would take delight in Your law, let him(her) meditate on it day and night, so that whatever he(she) does will prosper. ~Amen (Psalm 1:1-3)

NOTES:

August 12

Category: Anger
Verse: Psalm 86:15
Focus: Pray for your child to be slow to anger.

Gracious God, would You teach _____ how to become like You: compassionate and gracious, help _____ be slow to anger, and abounding in love and faithfulness. ~Amen (Psalm 86:15)

NOTES:

August 13

Category: Wisdom
Verse: 1 Kings 16:7,11
Focus: Pray for your child to have a discerning heart.

Gracious God, I pray that You would give _____ a wise and discerning heart so that he(she) can distinguish between right and wrong. ~Amen (1 Kings 16:7, 11)

NOTES:

August 14

Category: Missions/Others
Verse: Proverbs 31:20
Focus: Pray for your child to be compassionate.

Heavenly Father, I pray that _____ would open his(her) arms to the poor and extend his(her) hands to the needy. ~Amen (Proverbs 31:20)

NOTES:

August 15

Category: Friendship
Verse: Proverbs 12:18 & 18:21
Focus: Pray for your child's word choices.

Gracious God, remind _____ that reckless words pierce like a sword, but the tongue of the wise brings healing (Proverbs 12:18). Also, remind _____ that the tongue has the power of life and death. ~Amen (Proverbs 18:21)

NOTES:

August 16

Category: School/Character
Verse: 2 Corinthians 5:7
Focus: Pray for your child's teacher.

Dear God, may (teacher's name)_____ be a person
who walks by faith and not by sight. ~Amen (2 Corinthians 5:7)

NOTES:

August 17

Category: Soul
Verse: Deuteronomy 4:39
Focus: Pray for your child to believe in God.

Heavenly Father, may _____ acknowledge and take to heart that
You are God in heaven above and on earth below. May he(she)
believe that there is no other God but You. ~Amen
(Deuteronomy 4:39)

NOTES:

August 18

Category: Anxiety
Verse: Romans 8:26
Focus: Pray for your child's prayer life.

Heavenly Father, I pray that Your Spirit will help _____ in his(her) weaknesses. When _____ doesn't know how what to pray for, may Your Spirit intercede for him(her), with groans that words cannot express. ~Amen (Romans 8:26)

NOTES:

August 19

Category: Temptation
Verse: 1 Corinthians 10:13
Focus: Pray for your child's stressful times.

My Lord and God, because You are faithful, I ask that You not let _____ be tempted beyond what he(she) can bear, but when _____ is tempted, cause him(her) to look to You for the way out only You can provide, please give _____ strength to stand up under the stress of temptation. ~Amen (1 Corinthians 10:13)

NOTES:

August 20

Category: Friendship
Verse: Proverbs 20:3
Focus: Pray for your child to be agreeable.

Heavenly Father, help _____ not be a fool who is quick to quarrel, remind him(her) that it is to a person's honor to avoid strife. ~Amen (Proverbs 20:3)

NOTES:

August 21

Category: Anxiety
Verse: Deuteronomy 3:12, 27
Focus: Pray for your child to rest in God.

Heavenly Father, may _____ rest secure in You, for You shield him(her) all day long; may _____ rest between Your shoulders; Eternal God, be _____'s refuge and put Your everlasting arms underneath him(her). Amen (Deuteronomy 3: 12, 27)

NOTES:

August 22

Category: Faithful Living
Verse: Ephesians 3:16-17a
Focus: Pray for your child's inner strength.

I pray that out of Your glorious riches, Lord, You would strengthen _____ with power through Your Spirit in his(her) inner being, so that Christ may dwell in _____'s heart through faith. ~Amen (Ephesians 3:16-17a)

NOTES:

August 23

Category: Temptation
Verse: Nehemiah 8:10b
Focus: Pray for your child to be joyful.

Oh, God, may the joy of You, Lord, be _____'s strength. ~Amen (Nehemiah 8:10b)

NOTES:

August 24

Category: Mind & Body
Verse: 1 Peter 5:8-9
Focus: Pray for your child's faith to be firm.

Heavenly Father, make _____ self-controlled and alert. Remind him(her) that our enemy the Devil prowls around like a roaring lion looking for someone to devour. Help _____ to resist him and to stand firm in the faith. ~Amen (1 Peter 5:8-9)

NOTES:

August 25

Category: Work Ethic
Verse: Colossians 3:20-21
Focus: A parent's prayer.

Heavenly Father, teach _____ to obey us (his/her parents) in everything, for this pleases You, Lord. Do not let us do or say anything that would embitter or discourage _____. ~Amen (Colossians 3:20-21)

NOTES:

August 26

Category: Family
Verse: Ephesians 4:32
Focus: Pray for sibling relationships.

Gracious God, show _____ and his(her) siblings how to be kind and compassionate to one another, forgiving each other, just as You have forgiven each of them. ~Amen (Ephesians 4:32)

NOTES:

August 27

Category: Future
Verse: Proverbs 19:21
Focus: Pray for your child's future.

Father, no matter what _____ is planning in his(her) heart, let Your purpose prevail in _____'s life. ~Amen (Proverbs 19:21)

NOTES:

August 28

Category: Heart
Verse: John 13:34-35
Focus: Pray for your child to be compassionate.

Dear Lord, I pray that _____ would love others in the same way that You love people. Help his(her) friends to see ____'s compassion to others and know that he(she) is Your disciple. ~Amen (John 13:34-35 NIV)

NOTES:

August 29

Category: Life Issues
Verse: Psalm 18:1-2
Focus: Pray for your child's driving skills.

Lord, I ask that You would be _____'s strength when he(she) drives. Be _____'s rock; form a fortress around him(her) as he(she) travels. Be _____'s deliverer when danger approaches and provide Your shield and horn when _____ is not even aware that he(she) needs protection. Be the stronghold in _____'s life and grant traveling mercies upon him(her). ~Amen (Psalm 18:1-2)

NOTES:

August 30

Category: Love God's Word
Verse: Deuteronomy 6:4-5
Focus: Pray for your child's heart, soul, and strength.

Heavenly Father, may _____ love You, Lord God, with all his(her) heart, love You with all his(her) soul and love You with all his(her) strength. ~Amen (Deuteronomy 6:4-5)

NOTES:

August 31

Category: Future
Verse: Jeremiah 10:23
Focus: Pray for your child's path in life.

Gracious God, may_____ realize that his(her) life is not his(her) own, may _____ look to You to direct his(her) steps. ~Amen (Jeremiah 10:23)

NOTES:

September

Nothing is too difficult for God. Bring your prayers to Him knowing He loves you and wants His best for you and your children.

September 1

Category: Temptation
Verse: Romans 6:12-13
Focus: Pray for your child's self control.

Lord, I pray that _____ would not let sin control the way he(she) lives, give him(her) strength so as not to give in to sinful desires. Block _____ from using any part of his(her) body as an instrument of evil to serve sin. Instead, may _____ give him(herself) completely to God and bring glory to You, Lord. ~Amen (Romans 6:12-13 NLT)

NOTES:

September 2

Category: Others
Verse: Zechariah 7:9
Focus: Pray for your child's compassion.

Heavenly Father, may _____ judge fairly, may he(she) show mercy and kindness to others, especially to widows and orphans, foreigners and poor people, those in great need. ~Amen (Zechariah 7:9 NLT)

NOTES:

September 3

Category: Faithful Living
Verse: Micah 6:8
Focus: Pray for your child to be humble.

May _____ realize what You, Lord, require of a person: help _____ to act justly, and to love mercy, and to walk humbly with You, God. ~Amen (Micah 6:8)

NOTES:

September 4

Category: Character
Verse: Psalm 119:9-11
Focus: Pray for your child to live by God's Word.

Lord, help _____ ponder how a young person can keep his(her) ways pure. Cause _____ to live according to Your Word, may _____ seek You with all his(her) heart; don't let _____ stray from Your commands, but instead hide Your Word in his(her) heart so that he(she) may not sin against You. ~Amen (Psalm 119:9-11)

NOTES:

September 5

Category: Soul
Verse: Matthew 4:4
Focus: Pray for your child to know God's Word.

Heavenly Father, may _____ not live on bread alone, but on every Word that comes from the mouth of God. ~Amen (Matthew 4:4)

NOTES:

September 6

Category: Service
Verse: Ephesians 4:11-16
Focus: Pray for your child's gifts and talents.

Gracious God, You made some people apostles, some prophets, some evangelists, and some pastors and teachers. Show _____ where he(she) fits into Your divine arrangement, and let _____ use his(her) gifts to prepare Your people for works of service, so that the body of Christ may be built up in love. ~Amen (Ephesians 4:11-16)

NOTES:

September 7

Category: Service
Verse: Matthew 20:26-28
Focus: Pray for your child to serve others.

Heavenly Father, teach _____ that if he(she) wants to become great, he(she) must be a servant. If _____ wants to be first, he(she) must be a slave--just as the Son of Man did not come to be served, but to serve, and to give His life as a ransom for many. ~Amen (Matthew 20:26-28)

NOTES:

September 8

Category: Others
Verse: Hebrews 13:2-3
Focus: Pray for your child to be hospitable.

Gracious God, do not let _____ forget to entertain strangers, for by doing so some have entertained angels without knowing it. ~Amen (Hebrews 13:2-3)

NOTES:

September 9

Category: Faithful Living
Verse: Psalm 37:4-5
Focus: Pray the your child will delight in the Lord.

Cause _____ to delight in You, Lord. Would You bless him(her) with the desires of his(her) heart. Let _____ commit everything he(she) does to You, and trust in You, because You will help him(her). ~Amen (Psalm 37:4-5 NLT)

NOTES:

September 10

Category: Anxiety
Verse: Psalm 40:1-3
Focus: Pray for a child under pressure or in crisis.

Heavenly Father, help _____ wait patiently for Your help.
You have promised to hear his(her) cry. Lift _____ out of the pit of
despair, out of the mud and the mire. Set _____'s feet on solid ground
and steady him(her) as he(she) walks along. Give _____ a new song
to sing, a hymn of praise to You, God. ~Amen. (Psalms 40:1-3 NLT)

NOTES:

September 11

Category: Soul
Verse: Psalm 31:14-15
Focus: Pray for your child to trust God.

Gracious Father, would You cause _____ to put his(her) trust in
You, O Lord; let _____ say, "You are my God. My times and my
days are in Your hands." ~Amen (Psalm 31:14-15)

NOTES:

September 12

Category: Future
Verse: Psalm 138:8
Focus: Pray for your child's life purpose.

Lord, I pray and ask that You would fulfill Your purpose for
_____; may he(she) know that Your steadfast love that endures
forever. ~Amen (Psalm 138:8 ESV)

NOTES:

September 13

Category: Anxiety
Verse: Psalm 27:1b
Focus: Prayer for a fearful child.

Oh Lord, may _____ say, "God, You are the strength of my life; of
whom shall I be afraid?" ~Amen (Psalm 27:1b)

NOTES:

September 14

Category: Service/Family
Verse: Ephesians 4:1-2
Focus: Pray for your child to have patience.

Lord, I pray for _____, that he(she) would walk in a manner worthy of You. Give _____ the humility and gentleness, along with the patience he(she) needs to bear with others in love. ~Amen (Ephesians 4:1-2 ESV)

NOTES:

September 15

Category: Temptation
Verse: Ephesians 4:14-15
Focus: Pray for your child to grow in Christ.

God, I ask that You would protect _____ from being tossed to and fro by waves and carried about by every wind of doctrine, or by human cunning, or by craftiness in deceitful schemes. Help _____ to grow in Christ. ~Amen (Ephesians 4:14-15 ESV)

NOTES:

September 16

Category: Character/Friendship
Verse: Ephesians 5:4
Focus: Pray for your child to be thankful.

Lord, would You inspire _____ to put away filthiness and foolish talk, as well as crude joking, which are out of place; instead let _____ be filled with thanksgiving. ~Amen (Ephesians 5:4 ESV)

NOTES:

September 17

Category: Future
Verse: Psalm 90:12
Focus: Pray for your child's time management.

Gracious God, teach _____ to make the most of his(her) time, help him(her) grow in wisdom. ~Amen (Psalm 90:12 NLT)

NOTES:

September 18

Category: Work Ethic
Verse: Galatians 6:5
Focus: Pray for your child to enjoy working.

Heavenly Father, I pray that _____ would learn responsibility and how to carry him(her) own load. ~Amen (Galatians 6:5 HCSB)

NOTES:

September 19

Category: Mind & body
Verse: 1 Peter 3:3-4
Focus: Pray for your child's self esteem.

Dear Lord, help _____ not be concerned about the outward beauty of fancy hairstyles, expensive jewelry, or beautiful clothes. Instead, may he(she) clothe him(her)self with the beauty that comes from within, the unfading beauty of a gentle and quiet spirit, which is so precious to God. ~Amen (1 Peter 3:3-4 NLT)

NOTES:

September 20

Category: Heart
Verse: Ezra 7:10
Focus: Pray for your child to study God's Word.

Dear God, may _____ be like Ezra, and set his(her) heart to study the Law of the Lord, and to do it, and to teach it. ~Amen (Ezra 7:10 ESV)

NOTES:

September 21

Category: Temptation
Verse: Ephesians 6:9-10
Focus: Pray for your child to put on the armor of God.

God, I pray that _____ would be strong in You, Lord and in Your mighty power. May _____ put on the full armor of God so that he(she) can take a stand against the Devils' schemes. ~Amen (Ephesians 6:9-10)

NOTES:

September 22

Category: Life Issues
Verse: 1 Timothy 6:18
Focus: Pray for your child to be generous.

Gracious God, I pray that ____ would learn to use their money to do good. May he(she) be rich in good works and generous to those in need, always ready to share with others. ~Amen
(1 Timothy 6:18 NLT)

NOTES:

September 23

Category: Future
Verse: Proverbs 16:3
Focus: Pray for your child's success.

Gracious God, help _____ commit to You Lord whatever he(she) does so that _____'s plans will succeed. ~Amen (Proverbs 16:3)

NOTES:

September 24

Category: Faithful Living
Verse: Deuteronomy 6:2
Focus: Pray for your child's longevity.

Heavenly Father, may _____ and his(her) children fear You as Lord God as long as he(she) lives. Help _____ keep Your decrees and commands so that he(she) may enjoy long life. ~Amen
(Deuteronomy 6:2)

NOTES:

September 25

Category: Mind & Body
Verse: 1 Corinthians 6:19-20
Focus: Pray that your child will honor God with their body.

Gracious God, remind _____ that his(her) body is a temple of the Holy Spirit, which is in him(her). Remind _____ that he(she) is not his(her) own, that You bought him(her) with a price. May _____ honor You with his(her) body. ~Amen
(1 Corinthians 6:19-20)

NOTES:

September 26

Category: Blessing
Verse: Galatians 5:22-23
Focus: Pray the fruit of the Spirit for your child.

God, I ask that You remove the unpleasant things in _____'s heart and fill his(her) heart instead with the fruits of Your Spirit: fill _____ with love and joy and peace, fill _____ with patience and kindness and goodness, fill _____ with gentleness, self-control, and above all else, fill _____ with love. ~Amen (Galatians 5:22-23)

NOTES:

September 27

Category: Anxiety
Verse: Psalm 147:3
Focus: Pray for your child's heart.

Lord, I pray that You would heal _____ when he(she) is brokenhearted and bind up his(her) wounds. ~Amen (Psalm 147:3)

NOTES:

September 28

Category: Prodigal
Verse: Psalm 90:8,12
Focus: Pray for your child's struggles.

You, O Lord, spread out _____'s sins, his(her) secret sins, and You see them all. When _____ stumbles, teach him(her) to make the most of his(her) time so that he(she) may grow in wisdom. ~Amen (Psalm 90:8, 12 NLT)

NOTES:

September 29

Category: Anger
Verse: Ephesians 4:22-27
Focus: Pray for a transformed heart and a new attitude for your child.

Gracious God, show _____ how to put off his(her) old self, which is being corrupted by its deceitful desires, and make _____ new in the attitude of his(her) mind. Cause _____ to put off falsehood and to speak truthfully, and to refrain from sin when he(she) is angry. Above all, do not let _____ do anything that would give the devil a foothold in his(her) life. ~Amen (Ephesians 4:22-27)

NOTES:

September 30

Category: Blessing
Verse: Philippians 4:6-7
Focus: Pray for your child's anxiety.

Lord, I ask that You not let _____ be anxious about anything, but in everything, through prayer and petition, with thanksgiving, let _____ remember to present their requests to You. And may Your peace, which transcends all understanding, guard _____'s heart and mind in Christ Jesus. ~Amen (Philippians 4:6-7)

NOTES:

October

The Father welcomes you into prayer as you pray His holy Word back to Him. Have confidence as you approach His throne and turn your child over to Him in prayer.

October 1

Category: Protection
Verse: Psalm 18:16
Focus: Pray for a child in crisis.

Lord, would You reach down from on high and take hold of _____, draw him(her) out of deep waters. ~Amen (Psalm 18:16)

NOTES:

October 2

Category: Friendship
Verse: Proverbs 11:13
Focus: Pray for your child to be a trustworthy friend.

Lord, I pray that _____ would not gossip, because gossip betrays a confidence, but that _____ would be a trustworthy person who is able to keep a confidence. ~Amen (Proverbs 11:13)

NOTES:

October 3

Category: School
Verse: Colossians 2:8
Focus: Pray for your child's principles.

Heavenly Father, do not let any teacher take _____ captive through hollow and deceptive philosophy, which depends on human tradition and the basic principles of this world rather than on Christ. ~Amen (Colossians 2:8)

NOTES:

October 4

Category: Faith
Verse: 2 Peter 3:18
Focus: Pray for your child to know God and be full of grace.

Gracious God, I pray that _____ would grow in the grace and knowledge of his(her) Lord and Savior Jesus Christ. To You, O God, be glory both now and forever! ~Amen. (2 Peter 3:18)

NOTES:

October 5

Category: Soul/Blessing
Verse: Jeremiah 32:39-40
Focus: Pray for God's goodness in your child's life.

Heavenly Father, would You count _____ as one of Your people, and be his(her) God. Give _____ singleness of heart and action, so the he(she) will always fear You for his(her) own good and for the good of his(her) children. Make an everlasting covenant with _____. Never stop doing good to him(her), and inspire _____ to fear You so that he(she) will never turn away from You. ~Amen (Jeremiah 32:39-40)

NOTES:

October 6

Category: Missions
Verse: 2 Timothy 4:2-5
Focus: Pray for your child to stand up for God's Word.

Gracious God, let _____ preach the Word and be prepared,
in season and out of season; may _____ correct, rebuke, and
encourage--with great patience and careful instruction. When the
time comes that people do not put up with the sound doctrine
but listen to teachers who say what their itching ears want to hear,
don't let _____ lose heart. Let him(her) keep his(her) head in all
situations, endure hardships, and do the work of an evangelist.
~Amen (2 Timothy 4:2-5)

NOTES:

October 7

Category: Friendship
Verse: 1 Thessalonians 5:15
Focus: Pray for your child to have patience.

Dear Lord, I pray _____ would develop into a patient person,
attentive to individual needs. When others get on his(her) nerves,
may ____ be careful not to snap at them but to look for the best in
each other, and bring out the best in them. ~Amen
(1 Thessalonians 5:15 MSG)

NOTES:

October 8

Category: Temptation
Verse: Psalm 10:4
Focus: Pray for God to guard your child against pride.

Please guard _____ against pride that stops him(her) from seeking You out, Lord; in all _____'s thoughts help him(her) make room for You, God. ~Amen (Psalm 10:4)

NOTES:

October 9

Category: Faithful Living
Verse: Psalm 25:4-5
Focus: Pray for your child to follow God.

Gracious God, I pray that You would show _____ the path where he(she) should walk, O Lord, point out the right road for him(her) to follow. Lead _____ by Your truth and teach him(her), for You are the God who saves _____. All day long, may he(she) put his(her) hope in You. ~Amen (Psalm 25:4-5 NLT)

NOTES:

October 10

Category: Character
Verse: Proverbs 3:3
Focus: Pray for your child to be kind.

Lord, I pray that _____ will not let kindness and truth leave
him(her), but that _____ would bind them around his(her) neck
and write them on the tablet of his(her) heart ~Amen
(Proverbs 3:3 NASB)

NOTES:

October 11

Category: Friendship
Verse: Luke 6:36-38
Focus: Pray for your child to be giving.

Loving God, I pray that _____ would be merciful, just as You,
his(her) Father is merciful. Help _____ not to be judgmental
or condemning but forgiving. May _____ be giving -- a good
measure, pressed down, shaken together, running over and poured
into his(her) lap. Remind _____ that with the measure he(she)
uses, that same measure will be used with him(her). ~Amen
(Luke 6:36-38)

NOTES:

October 12

Category: Character
Verse: Psalm 33:20-22
Focus: Pray a blessing over your child.

May _____'s soul wait for You, Lord; You are _____'s help and shield. May _____'s heart be glad in You and trust in Your holy name. May Your steadfast love, O Lord, be upon _____, help him(her) hope in You. ~Amen (Psalm 33:20-22 ESV)

NOTES:

October 13

Category: Character
Verse: Psalm 34:13-14
Focus: Pray for your child to be honest.

Heavenly Father, help _____ to watch his(her) tongue! Keep his(her) lips from telling lies! Help _____ turn away from evil and do good. May he(she) work hard at living in peace with others. ~Amen (Psalm 34:13-14 NLT)

NOTES:

October 14

Category: School
Verse: Psalm 4:8
Focus: Pray for your child's sleep.

Gracious God, let _____ lie down and sleep in peace. (Psalm 4:8)
For a little one, for a child getting ready for to a school schedule,
for those who are sick or in need of rest, God, please give _____ a
restful nights sleep. ~Amen (Psalm 4:8)

NOTES:

October 15

Category: Others/Service
Verse: 1 Peter 4:8-11
Focus: Pray for your child to serve others.

Heavenly Father, above all, may _____ love others deeply, because
love covers a multitude of sins. May _____ use whatever gifts
he(she) has received to serve others, faithfully administering Your
grace in its various forms. May _____ serve with the strength
You provide, so that in all things You, O Lord, will be praised and
receive and glory. ~Amen (1 Peter 4:8-11)

NOTES:

October 16

Category: Anxiety
Verse: Isaiah 43:1-2
Focus: Pray for your child in a crisis.

Heavenly Father, may _____ not be fearful. Thank You that
You have redeemed _____ and that You call him(her) by name,
_____ is Yours. When he(she) passes through the water (trials,
temptations, peer pressure, heartbreak, suffering, etc), be with
_____. When he(she) passes through the rivers, do not let them
sweep over him(her). When he(she) walks through fire, do not let
_____ be burned. ~Amen (Isaiah 43:1-2)

NOTES:

October 17

Category: Character
Verse: 1 John 3:7
Focus: Pray for your child to be discerning.

Today, gracious God, do not let anyone lead _____ astray. Instead
help him(her) to do what is righteous rather than what is sinful.
~Amen (1 John 3:7)

NOTES:

October 18

Category: Anxiety
Verse: Psalm 56:3-4
Focus: Pray for your child to trust God.

Heavenly Father, when _____ feels afraid, remind him(her) to put his(her) trust in You; may _____ praise You for Your promises. ~Amen (Psalm 56:3-4)

NOTES:

October 19

Category: Friendship
Verse: James 4:4
Focus: Pray for your child to be a friend of God.

Heavenly Father, let _____ seek friendship with You rather than with the world, remembering that anyone who chooses to be a friend of the world becomes Your enemy. ~Amen (James 4:4)

NOTES:

October 20

Category: School/Friendship
Verse: Proverbs 16:28
Focus: Pray for your child to have integrity.

Gracious God, I pray that _____ wouldn't participate in gossip or exclude his(her) peers, remind him(her) that a troublemaker plants seeds of strife, and a gossip separates the best of friends. ~Amen (Proverbs 16:28 NLT)

NOTES:

October 21

Category: Blessing
Verse: Isaiah 11:5
Focus: Pray for your child's righteousness.

Father, may righteousness be _____'s belt, and faithfulness the sash around _____'s waist. ~Amen (Isaiah 11:5)

NOTES:

October 22

Category: Parent/Child Relationship
Verse: Hebrews 12:5-10
Focus: Pray for your relationship with your child.

Heavenly Father, may _____ recognize that when we, his(her) parents, discipline him(her), it means that we love him(her) and that he(she) belongs to our family, just as You discipline those You love, those You accept as Your sons and daughters. May _____ respect us when we discipline him(her), realizing that we are doing our best and that we ourselves are submitting to Your discipline, which is for our good. ~Amen (Hebrews 12:5-10)

NOTES:

October 23

Category: Anger
Verse: Matthew 5:22-24
Focus: Pray for your child to control their anger.

Gracious God, I pray that You would help _____ control his(her) anger, since anyone who is angry with a brother will be subject to judgment. If _____ holds anything against one of his(her) siblings, would You prompt him(her) to go and be reconciled so that he(she) may have fellowship with You. ~Amen (Matthew 5:22-24)

NOTES:

October 24

Category: Anger
Verse: James 1:19-20
Focus: Pray for your child's attitude.

Heavenly Father, may _____ be quick to listen, may he(she) be slow to speak and slow to become angry. Remind _____ that his(her) anger does not bring about the righteous life that God desires. ~Amen (James 1:19-20)

NOTES:

October 25

Category: Prodigal
Verse: Isaiah 54:10
Focus: Pray for your child's faith.

Heavenly Father, though the mountains be shaken and the hills be removed, remind _____ of Your unfailing love which will not be shaken. Remind _____ of Your compassion for him(her). ~Amen (Isaiah 54:10)

NOTES:

October 26

Category: Faith
Verse: 1 John 3:18
Focus: Pray for your child to love others.

Heavenly Father, I pray that _____ will love not just with words or tongue, but with actions and in truth. ~Amen (1 John 3:18)

NOTES:

October 27

Category: Love God's Word
Verse: Philippians 1:9-11
Focus: Pray for insight for your child.

Wonderful Father, this is my prayer: that _____'s love may abound more and more in knowledge and depth of insight, may _____ be able to discern what is best and may he(she) be pure and blameless until the day of Christ; I pray that _____ will be filled with the fruit of righteousness that comes through Jesus Christ -- to the glory and praise of God. ~Amen (Philippians 1:9-11)

NOTES:

October 28

Category: Soul
Verse: 1 Thessalonians 1:4-5
Focus: Pray for your child to be fully convinced of God.

Lord, I ask that You choose _____. Bring the gospel to him(her) not just with words, but through power and Your Holy Spirit, so that _____ will be fully convinced of his(her) need of You, Lord. ~Amen (1 Thessalonians 1:4-5)

NOTES:

October 29

Category: Blessing
Verse: Psalm 29:11
Focus: Pray for peace for your child.

Dear God, I pray that You would give _____ strength, bless him(her) with peace. ~Amen. (Psalm 29:11)

NOTES:

October 30

Category: School
Verse: John 14:1
Focus: Pray for the staff at your child's school.

Lord, I pray the staff at _____ school will not let their hearts be troubled, but believe in You, God, and in Your Son Jesus Christ. ~Amen (John 14:1 NASB)

NOTES:

October 31

Category: Anger
Verse: Galatians 5:26, 1 Peter 5:5
Focus: Pray for your child's character.

My God, don't let _____ become conceited, may he(she) not provoke or envy others. Instead, may he(she) clothe him(her)self in humility toward others.~Amen (Galatians 5:26, 1 Peter 5:5)

NOTES:

November

Prayer is faith-infused intercession. Be persistent in prayer for your child and trust God to answer.

November 1

Category: Soul
Verse: 1 John 3:23
Focus: Pray for your child to love others and be humble.

My God, don't let _____ become conceited, may he(she) not provoke or envy others. ~Amen (Galatians 5:26)

NOTES:

November 2

Category: Character
Verse: Ephesians 4:25
Focus: Pray for your child to be honest and truthful.

Gracious God, I pray that You would help _____ to put off falsehood, and speak truthfully to his(her) friends, for we are all members of one body. ~Amen (Ephesians 4:25)

NOTES:

November 3

Category: Character
Verse: Psalm 26:2-3
Focus: Pray for your child to be introspective.

Gracious God, I ask that You would test, _____, O Lord, and try _____, examine his(her) heart and mind; with Your love ever before _____, may he(she) continually walk in Your truth. ~Amen (Psalm 26:2-3)

NOTES:

November 4

Category: Life Issues
Verse: Proverbs 13:11, 23:4
Focus: Pray for your child to have wisdom dealing with money.

Dear God, help _____ understand that the one who gathers money little by little makes it grow. Help _____ not to wear himself(herself) out trying to get rich; instead grow in _____ self-control so that he(she) can restrain himself(herself). ~Amen (Proverbs 13:11, 23:4)

NOTES:

November 5

Category: Faithful Living
Verse: 1 Chronicles 28:9
Focus: Pray for your child's heart.

Heavenly Father, I pray that _____ acknowledge You, Father God, and serve You with wholehearted devotion, and with a willing mind. Remind _____ that You search every heart and understand every motive behind his(her) thoughts. May _____ seek You, for Your Word says, then he(she) will be found by You. ~Amen (1 Chronicles 28:9)

NOTES:

November 6

Category: Faith
Verse: Deuteronomy 31:6
Focus: Pray for your child to lean on God.

O God, I pray that _____ would be strong and take courage.
Don't let him(her) be intimidated; don't let him(her) even give it a
second thought because You, O God, are striding ahead of _____.
You are right there with _____, remind him(her) You won't let
him(her) down, You won't leave him(her). ~Amen
(Deuteronomy 3:6 MSG)

NOTES:

November 7

Category: Temptation
Verse: Psalm 119:29-32
Focus: Pray for your child's path in life.

Heavenly Father, keep _____ from deceitful ways. Help him(her)
to choose the way of truth and to set his(her) heart on Your laws,
so that he(she) will not be put to shame. May _____ run in the
path of Your commands, and may he(she) realize that You set
his(her) heart free. ~Amen (Psalm 119:29-32)

NOTES:

November 8

Category: Anxiety
Verse: Isaiah 26:3-4a
Focus: Pray for your child to trust God.

Gracious God, I pray that You would keep _____ in perfect peace, because he(she) trusts in You. May _____ trust in You, Lord, forever. ~Amen (Isaiah 26:3-4a)

NOTES:

November 9

Category: Blessing
Verse: Psalm 119:30
Focus: Pray for your child to have a transformed heart.

Dear God, cause _____ to choose the way of truth, and may he(she) set his(her) heart on Your laws. ~Amen (Psalm 119:30)

NOTES:

November 10

Category: Soul
Verse: 2 Chronicles 7:14
Focus: Pray for your child to seek God.

Heavenly Father, cause _____, who is called by Your name, to humble himself(herself) and pray, cause _____ to seek Your face and to turn from his(her) wicked ways, so that You will hear _____ and forgive his(her) sin. ~Amen (2 Chronicles 7:14)

NOTES:

November 11

Category: Faithful Living
Verse: 1 John 3:1
Focus: Pray for your child to remember he(she) is God's child.

Dear Lord, remind _____ how great is the love You have lavished on him(her), _____ is called a child of God, and that is what _____ is: Your child. ~Amen (1 John 3:1)

NOTES:

November 12

Category: Temptation
Verse: 2 Corinthians 2:11
Focus: Pray for your child to guard their mind.

Holy Father, I pray that _____ will not unwittingly give Satan an opening for yet more mischief; help him(her) not be oblivious to his sly ways. ~Amen (2 Corinthians 2:1 MSG)

NOTES:

November 13

Category: Blessing
Verse: Exodus 20:3-17
Focus: Pray the 10 Commandments for your child.

Good and Gracious God, I ask today that _____ have no other gods before You; may he(she) not make any idols for himself(herself); may _____ remember the Sabbath day and keep it holy; may he(she) honor his(her) father and mother; may _____ not murder; may he(she) not commit adultery; may _____ not steal; may he(she) not bear false witness against his(her) neighbor; may he(she) not covet others possessions; may _____ love You with all his(her) heart, mind, soul, and strength. ~Amen (Exodus 20:3-17)

NOTES:

November 14

Category: Service
Verse: Deuteronomy 10:12-13a
Focus: Pray for your child's walk with God.

Lord God, I pray that You would show _____ what You require of him(her): may _____ fear You, Lord God, may _____ walk in all Your ways, may he(she) love You, and serve You Lord, with all his(her) heart and with all his(her) soul, and may _____ keep the commandments and statutes of the Lord. ~Amen (Deuteronomy 10:12-13a)

NOTES:

November 15

Category: Love God's Word
Verse: Proverbs 7:2-3
Focus: Pray for your child to treasure God's Word.

Heavenly Father, may _____ treasure Your instructions; may he(she) do what You say so he(she) will live well. Your teaching is precious as eyesight, may _____ guard it! May _____ write it out on the back of his(her) hands and etch it on the chambers of his(her) heart. ~Amen (Proverbs 7:2-3 MSG)

NOTES:

November 16

Category: Temptation
Verse: Ephesians 6:14
Focus: Pray for your child to stand firm in the face of adversity.

Holy, all-powerful God, I pray that You would enable _____ to stand firm with the belt of truth buckled around his(her) waist, with the breastplate of righteousness in place. ~Amen (Ephesians 6:14)

NOTES:

November 17

Category: Love God's Word
Verse: Nahum 1:7
Focus: Pray for your child to know that God cares and see Him as a refuge.

Heavenly Father, help _____ know that You are good, that You are a refuge in times of trouble, for You care for those who trust You. ~Amen (Nahum 1:7)

NOTES:

November 18

Category: Anxiety
Verse: Lamentations 3:22-23
Focus: Pray for your child to know God's faithfulness.

Dear Lord, remind _____ that because of Your great love, he(she) is not consumed; remind _____ that Your compassion never fails, it is new every morning. Great is Your faithfulness to _____, O Lord! ~Amen (Lamentations 3:22-23)

NOTES:

November 19

Category: Blessing
Verse: Proverbs 16:20
Focus: Pray for your child to trust God and be teachable.

Lord, I pray that _____ would give heed to Your instruction and prosper; I ask that You bless _____when he(she) trusts in, You, Lord. ~Amen (Proverbs 16:20)

NOTES:

November 20

Category: Prodigal
Verse: Psalm 91
Focus: Pray Psalm 91 for your child.

Heavenly Father, let _____ dwell in the shelter of the Most High and rest in the shadow of the Almighty. Be _____'s refuge, his(her) fortress, be _____'s covering, his(her) shield. Do not let him(her) fear the terror of the night,nor any type of plague or sickness. Do not let any harm or disaster come near _____. Command Your angels to guard _____ in all his(her) ways and keep him(her) from hurting himself(herself). When _____ calls on You, answer him(her). Be with _____ in trouble, deliver him(her), and honor him(her). Satisfy _____ with long life and show him(her) Your salvation. ~Amen (Psalm 91)

NOTES:

November 21

Category: Character
Verse: Proverbs 13:1
Focus: Pray for your child's character and wisdom, and for yourself as you parent.

Gracious God, I pray that _____ would be a wise child and accept his(her) parent's discipline, don't let _____ refuse to listen to correction. ~Amen (Proverbs 13:1 NLT)

NOTES:

November 22

Category: Love God's Word
Verse: 1 Peter 2:2
Focus: Pray for your child to crave God's Word.

Heavenly Father, may _____ be like a newborn baby, who craves the pure spiritual milk so that it will nourish his(her) soul and help him(her) grow up in his(her) salvation. ~Amen (1 Peter 2:2)

NOTES:

November 23

Category: Future
Verse: Proverbs 3:4
Focus: Pray for your child's favor.

Gracious God, I pray that _____ will win favor and a good name in the sight of You, God, and of men. ~Amen (Proverbs 3:4)

NOTES:

November 24

Category: Faithful Living
Verse: Acts 19:20
Focus: Pray for God's Word to influence your child.

Gracious God, I pray that Your message will move in _____'s life
and have a powerful effect. ~Amen (Acts 19:20 NLT)

NOTES:

November 25

Category: Soul
Verse: 1 Peter 1:14-15
Focus: Pray for your child to choose holiness and make good life
choices.

Heavenly Father, I pray that _____ would live as God's obedient
child. Help him(her) live for You and not satisfy his(her) own
desires, but rather help _____ to be holy in everything he(she)
does. ~Amen (1 Peter 1:14-15 NLT)

NOTES:

November 26

Category: Character
Verse: 2 Timothy 1:7-9
Focus: Pray for your child to have a spirit of power.

Lord, I pray that You would give _____ a spirit of power, of love and of self-discipline, keep him(her) from a spirit of timidity; for You have saved _____ and called him(her) to a holy life, by Your purpose and grace, given to _____ in Christ Jesus before the beginning of time. ~Amen (2 Timothy 1:7, 9)

NOTES:

November 27

Category: Soul
Verse: 1 John 2:15
Focus: Pray for your child's desires.

All-powerful God, I pray that _____ would not love the world's way, or love the world's goods. Help him(her) see that love with the world squeezes out love for You, Father. ~Amen (1 John 2:15 MSG)

NOTES:

November 28

Category: Character/Friendship
Verse: Proverbs 19:11
Focus: Pray for your child to have patience.

Heavenly Father, I pray that _____ would understand that a person's wisdom gives him(her) patience; may _____ see that it is to his(her) glory to overlook an offense. ~Amen (Proverbs 19:11)

NOTES:

November 29

Category: Faithful Living
Verse: Amos 5:14
Focus: Pray for your child to be kind.

Dear Lord, I pray that _____ would seek good, not evil, so that he(she) may live; Lord God Almighty, I ask that you be with _____. ~Amen (Amos 5:14)

NOTES:

November 30

Category: Soul
Verse: Matthew 22:37-39
Focus: Pray for your child to love others.

Lord God, I pray that _____ would love You, Lord, with all his(her) heart, and with all his(her) soul, and with all his(her) mind. And help _____ to love his(her) neighbors as himself(herself). ~Amen (Matthew 22:37-39)

NOTES:

December

God's Word is powerful. Place your hand on your child and pray Scripture over them asking that God will reveal Himself to them.

December 1

Category: Temptation/Friendship
Verse: Titus 2:6-8
Focus: Pray for your child to have integrity.

Gracious God, may _____, as a young person, be self-controlled. Help _____ be an example to others by doing what is good; help _____ have integrity and soundness of speech. ~Amen
(Titus 2:6-8 NLT)

NOTES:

December 2

Category: Heart
Verse: Psalm 86:11
Focus: Pray for your child's school year.

Gracious God, I pray that You would teach _____ Your way, O Lord, and help _____ walk in Your truth; give _____ an undivided heart that he(she) may fear Your name. ~Amen (Psalm 86:11)

NOTES:

December 3

Category: Blessing
Verse: Numbers 6:24-26
Focus: Pray a blessing over your child.

My dear _____, may the Lord bless you and keep you. May the Lord make his face shine upon you and be gracious to you. May the Lord look upon you with favor and give you peace. ~Amen (Numbers 6:4-26)

NOTES:

December 4

Category: Character
Verse: Proverbs 12:19-20
Focus: Pray for your child's honesty.

Holy Father, may _____ use truthful words so that they stand the test of time; expose any lies told by _____. May _____ have a heart filled with joy and peace instead of a deceitful heart. ~Amen (Proverbs 12:19-20 NLT)

NOTES:

December 5

Category: Praise
Verse: 1 Chronicles 29:11-13
Focus: Pray for your child to know God.

Gracious God, may _____ praise You, Lord, as the glorious God, the majestic God, as his(her) God who displays Your splendor both in heaven and on earth. Remind _____ that all things come from You (wealth and honor, talent and ability). May he(she) give thanks to You and praise Your name. ~Amen (1 Chronicles 29:11-13)

NOTES:

December 6

Category: Blessing
Verse: Psalm 23:1-3
Focus: Pray Psalm 23 for your child.

Lord God, I pray that _____ would be able to say that You are his(her) shepherd, may he(she) not be in want. Lead _____ beside quiet waters, restore his(her) soul; guide _____ in paths of righteousness, for Your name's sake. ~Amen (Psalm 23:1-3)

NOTES:

December 7

Category: Character
Verse: Romans 12:12
Focus: Pray for your child to have hope.

Father, my prayer for _____ is that he(she) will be joyful in hope, patient in affliction and faithful in prayer. ~Amen (Romans 12:12)

NOTES:

December 8

Category: Heart
Verse: Jeremiah 49:16
Focus: Pray for your child's heart.

Loving God, ever so gently, would You help _____ understand that the pride of his(her) heart has deceived him(her). ~Amen. (Jeremiah 49:16)

NOTES:

December 9

Category: Faithful Living
Verse: Psalm 55:22
Focus: Pray for your child to seek God.

Dear Lord, help _____ cast all his(her) cares on You, Lord, and remind _____ that You will sustain him(her), You will never let the righteous fall. ~Amen (Psalm 55:22)

NOTES:

December 10

Category: Temptation
Verse: 2 Peter 3:17-18
Focus: Pray for your child to grow in grace.

Heavenly Father, I pray that _____ would be on guard so as not to be carried away by the errors of wicked people and possibly lose his(her) own secure footing. May _____ grow in grace and knowledge of the Lord and Savior Jesus Christ. ~Amen (2 Peter 3:17-18)

NOTES:

December 11

Category: Praise
Verse: Isaiah 9:6
Focus: Pray for your child's heart this Christmas season.

Gracious God, teach _____ to praise You, God, as we celebrate this day that a child is born to us, a Son has been given to us; the government will rest on His shoulders. May _____ know You as his(her) Wonderful Counselor, the Mighty God, the Everlasting Father, and the Prince of Peace. ~Amen (Isaiah 9:6 NLT)

NOTES:

December 12

Category: Character
Verse: Hebrews 10:25
Focus: Pray for your child to enjoy church and be in fellowship.

Gracious God, teach _____ to praise You, God, as we celebrate this day that a child is born to us, a Son has been given to us; the government will rest on His shoulders. May _____ know You as his(her) Wonderful Counselor, the Mighty God, the Everlasting Father, and the Prince of Peace. ~Amen (Isaiah 9:6 NLT)

NOTES:

December 13

Category: Friendship/Future
Verse: Proverbs 4:23
Focus: Pray for your child's dating relationships.

Gracious God, I pray for _____ as they begin to form relationships with the opposite sex, help him(her) guard his(her) heart because it will affect everything he(she) does. ~Amen (Proverbs 4:23 NLT)

NOTES:

December 14

Category: Character
Verse: Philippians 4:8
Focus: Pray for the things on your child's heart and mind.

Today, Lord, I pray for _____ and the things he(she) thinks about. May _____ focus on whatever is true, whatever is honorable, whatever is just, whatever is pure, whatever is lovely, whatever is commendable, anything of excellence, anything worthy of praise, help _____ to think about these things. ~Amen (Philippians 4:8)

NOTES:

December 15

Category: Future
Verse: 1 Peter 5:7-8a
Focus: Pray for your child's teenage years.

Dear Lord, as _____ drives, help him(her) cast all his(her) anxieties on You, because You are for _____. Help _____ to be self-controlled and alert when he's(she's) behind the wheel. And for me Lord, help me cast my anxieties on You when _____ is driving the car. ~Amen (1 Peter 5:7-8a)

NOTES:

December 16

Category: Anger
Verse: Proverbs 15:1
Focus: Pray for your child's discernment.

Heavenly Father, may _____ learn the value of a soft answer that turns away wrath and the destruction of a harsh word that stirs up anger. ~Amen (Proverbs 15:1 ESV)

NOTES:

December 17

Category: Heart
Verse: Proverbs 14:30
Focus: Pray for your child's heart.

Gracious God, may _____ have a tranquil heart, which gives life to the flesh; and not envy, which makes the bones rot. ~Amen (Proverbs 14:30 ESV)

NOTES:

December 18

Category: Love God's Word
Verse: Psalm 19:10
Focus: Pray for your child to love Scripture.

Dear God, I pray that _____ would discover that Your Word is better than a diamond, better than a diamond set between emeralds. May he(she) like it better than red, ripe strawberries in the spring. ~Amen (Psalm 19:10 MSG)

NOTES:

December 19

Category: Character
Verse: Proverbs 30:8
Focus: Pray for your child to be honest.

Gracious God, would You remove far from _____ any falsehood and lying. ~Amen (Proverbs 30:8 ESV)

NOTES:

December 20

Category: Family
Verse: Romans 15:5, 7
Focus: Pray for your child to be a person of harmony.

Faithful God, would You give _____ patience and encouragement; help him(her) live in complete harmony with his(her) siblings, as is fitting for followers of Christ Jesus. Help _____ to accept others just as Christ has accepted him(her), so that You, God, will be given glory. ~Amen (Romans 15:5, 7)

NOTES:

December 21

Category: Soul
Verse: John 15:5,7,9,11
Focus: Pray for your child to count on God.

Heavenly Father, I pray that _____ would remember that You are the vine and he(she) is a branch. Help _____ abide in You and bear fruit; remind him(her) that without You he(she) can do nothing. May Your words abide in _____, may _____abide in Your love and there find Your complete joy. ~Amen (John 15:5,7,9,11)

NOTES:

December 22

Category: Anxiety
Verse: 2 Corinthians 1:3-4
Focus: Pray for comfort for your child.

Please bless _____ with comfort in times of trouble. ~Amen
(2 Corinthians 1:3-4)

NOTES:

December 23

Category: Anxiety
Verse: Psalm 61:2
Focus: Pray when your child is anxious.

Gracious God, when _____'s heart is overwhelmed, lead him(her)
to Yourself, the towering rock of safety. ~Amen (Psalm 61:2)

NOTES:

December 24

Category: Family
Verse: 2 Thessalonians 3:16
Focus: Pray peace for your child.

As a parent, God, I ask that You, the Lord of peace himself, bring me peace at all times, in every way. I know that You are with me, and with my children. ~Amen (2 Thes 3:16 ESV)

NOTES:

December 25

Category: Anxiety
Verse: Matthew 6:34
Focus: Pray for your child to rest in God.

Dear Lord, I pray that _____ would not worry about tomorrow, for tomorrow will bring enough worries of its own. ~Amen (Matthew 6:34 NIV)

NOTES:

December 26

Category: Mind and Body
Verse: Colossians 3:17
Focus: Pray for your child to put God first.

Gracious God, whatever _____ does, in word or deed, let him(her) do everything in the name of Jesus, giving thanks to You. ~Amen (Colossians 3:17 NIV)

NOTES:

December 27

Category: Faith
Verse: Philippians 3:8-9
Focus: Pray for your child to value their faith.

Holy Father, I pray that _____ would consider everything else worthless as compared with the infinite value of knowing Christ Jesus as his(her) Lord. For Christ's sake, may _____ discard everything else, counting it all as garbage, so that he(she) can gain Christ and become one with Him. Help _____ no longer count on his(her) own righteousness through obeying the law but realize he(she) become righteous through faith in Christ. ~Amen (Philippians 3:8-9 NLT)

NOTES:

December 28

Category: Faithful Living
Verse: Matthew 17:20
Focus: Pray for your child's faith.

Dear Lord, I pray You would give _____ faith the size of a mustard seed; when he(she) tell this mountain "Move from here to there", it will move; Help _____ realize that nothing will be impossible for You. ~Amen (Matthew 17:20 HCSB)

NOTES:

December 29

Category: Soul
Verse: Joshua 24:15
Focus: Pray for your child to choose God.

Holy Father, I pray that _____ would choose to say: As for me and my house, we will serve the Lord." (Joshua 24:15 ESV)

NOTES:

December 30

Category: Mind and Body
Verse: Hebrews 11:6
Focus: Pray for your child's faith.

Holy Father, I pray that _____ would understand it is impossible to please You apart from faith. May he(she) come to You and believe that You exist and know that You reward those who sincerely seek You. ~Amen (Hebrews 11:6 NLT)

NOTES:

December 31

Category: Character
Verse: Psalm 11:7
Focus: Pray for your child to love justice.

Dear Lord, just as You are righteous, I pray that _____ would long to be righteous. Just as You love justice, I pray that _____ would love justice and fight for it. ~Amen (Psalm 11:7 NIV)

NOTES:

Section 2
Bible Praying by Category

While daily Bible praying is vitally important, sometimes our children need specific prayers at specific times for specific areas of need. That's why we added this section. Every prayer from Section One is organized by category.

Our hope is that you will use this section to spend an extended time praying specifically for your child's friendships, character, anxiety, etc. You could also use this section to guide a prayer time during your small group. If you meet with others, take one section each time you are together and – as a community of faith – lift up your children and theirs!

All of the categories are listed here – and over the next several pages – in alphabetical order.

Anger	Future	Praise
Anxiety	Heart	Prodigal
Blessing	Life Issues	Protection
Character	Love God's Word	School
Church	Mind and Body	Service
Faith	Missions	Soul
Faithful Living	Others	Temptation
Family	Parent/Child	Thanks
Friendships	Relationship	Work Ethic

Anger

Pray for your child when he(she) is overcome by anger. Be persistent in prayer and expect God to intervene.

Psalm 86:15   Gracious God, would You teach _____ how to become like You: compassionate and gracious, help _____ be slow to anger, and abounding in love and faithfulness. ~Amen

Psalm 103:8   Dear Lord, may _____ be like You--compassionate and gracious, may _____ be slow to anger and abounding in love. ~Amen (NLT)

Proverbs 15:1   Heavenly Father, may _____ learn the value of a soft answer that turns away wrath and the destruction of a harsh word that stirs up anger. ~Amen (ESV)

Matthew 5:22-24   Gracious God, I pray that You would help _____ control his(her) anger, since anyone who is angry with a brother will be subject to judgment. If _____ holds anything against one of his(her) siblings, would You prompt him(her) to go and be reconciled so that he(she) may have fellowship with You. ~Amen

Galatians 5:26   My God, don't let _____ become conceited, may he(she) not provoke or envy others. ~Amen

Ephesians 4:22-27   Gracious God, show _____ how to put off his(her) old self, which is being corrupted by its deceitful desires, and make _____ new in the attitude of his(her) mind. Cause _____ to put off falsehood and to speak truthfully, and to refrain from sin when he(she) is angry. Above all, do not let _____ do anything that would give the devil a foothold in his(her) life. ~Amen

**Colossians
3:8-10**

Gracious God, may _____ get rid of any anger
or rage in his(her) life, help _____ also get rid
of any malicious behavior, slander, or dirty
language. Don't let _____ lie to others; instead may
_____ clothe himself(herself) with a brand new
nature that is continually being renewed as he(she)
learns more and more about Christ, who created
this new nature within _____. ~Amen (NLT)

**James
1:19-20**

Heavenly Father, may _____ be quick to listen, may
he(she) be slow to speak and slow to become angry.
Remind _____ that his(her) anger does not bring
about the righteous life that God desires. ~Amen

Anxiety

When your child is anxious, pray God's heart as it is revealed in Scripture.

Deuteronomy 3:12, 27	Heavenly Father, may _____ rest secure in You, for You shield him(her) all day long; may _____ rest between Your shoulders; Eternal God, be _____'s refuge and put Your everlasting arms underneath him(her). ~Amen
Joshua 1:9	Heavenly Father, enable _____ to be strong and very courageous. Be with him(her) when he(she) is afraid or discouraged and remind him(her) that You are with him(her) wherever he(she) goes. ~Amen (NLT)
Psalm 27:1b	Oh Lord, may _____ say, "God, You are the strength of my life; of whom shall I be afraid?" ~Amen
Psalm 42:6	O God, when _____'s soul is downcast, help him(her) remember You and put his(her) hope in You. ~Amen (ESV)
Psalm 56:3-4	Heavenly Father, when _____ feels afraid, remind him(her) to put his(her) trust in You; may _____ praise You for Your promises. ~Amen
Psalm 61:2	Gracious God, when _____'s heart is overwhelmed, lead him(her) to Yourself, the towering rock of safety. ~Amen
Psalm 147:3	Lord, I pray that You would heal _____ when he(she) is brokenhearted and bind up his(her) wounds. ~Amen

Isaiah 26:3-4a	Gracious God, I pray that You would keep _____ in perfect peace, because he(she) trusts in You. May _____ trust in You, Lord, forever. ~Amen
Isaiah 40:11	Lord, You have promised to feed Your flock like a shepherd. I pray that You will carry _____, Your lamb, in Your arms and hold him(her) close to Your heart. ~Amen (NLT)
Lamentations 3:22-23	Dear Lord, remind _____ that because of Your great love, he(she) is not consumed; remind _____ that Your compassion never fails, it is new every morning. Great is Your faithfulness to _____, O Lord! ~Amen
Matthew 5:4	God, would You bless _____ when he(she) mourns, for You promise to comfort him(her). ~Amen (NLT)
Matthew 6:34	Dear Lord, I pray that _____ would not worry about tomorrow, for tomorrow will bring enough worries of its own. ~Amen
Romans 8:26	Heavenly Father, I pray that Your Spirit will help _____ in his(her) weaknesses. When _____ doesn't know how what to pray for, may Your Spirit intercede for him(her), with groans that words cannot express. ~Amen
Romans 8:31	Gracious God, I pray that You would remind _____ that if You are for him(her), who can be against him(her)? ~Amen

Romans
8:35-39

Dear God, don't let anything separate _____ from Christ's love. Thank You that You love _____ even if he(she) is in trouble or experiences calamity, even if he(she) is persecuted or hungry or destitute or in danger or threatened with death, nothing can separate _____ from Your love, O God. Remind him(her) not to fear today or worry about tomorrow because he(she) has overwhelming victory through Christ. ~Amen (NLT)

2 Corinthians
1:3-4

Please, bless _____ with comfort, in times of trouble. ~Amen

James
1:2-4

Lord God, when trouble comes _____'s way, help him(her) see it as an opportunity for joy. When _____'s faith is tested, may his(her) endurance grow so that he(she) will be strong in character and ready for anything. ~Amen (NLT)

Blessing

Lay your hands on your child's head and pray Scripture upon him(her) as a holy blessing.

Exodus 20:3-17   Good and Gracious God, I ask today that _____ have no other gods before You; may he(she) not make any idols for himself(herself); may _____ remember the Sabbath day and keep it holy; may he(she) honor his(her) father and mother; may _____ not murder; may he(she) not commit adultery; may _____ not steal; may he(she) not bear false witness against his(her) neighbor; may he(she) not covet others possessions; may _____ love You with all his(her) heart, mind, soul, and strength. ~Amen

Numbers 6:24-26   My dear _____, may the Lord bless you and keep you. May the Lord make his face shine upon you and be gracious to you. May the Lord look upon you with favor and give you peace. ~Amen

Psalm 1:1-2   Gracious God, may _____ know the joys of those who do not follow the advice of the wicked, or stand around with sinners, or join in with scoffers. Instead, may _____ delight in doing everything You want, O Lord; day and night help _____ think about Your law. ~Amen (NLT)

Psalm 3:3   Gracious Father, be a shield, O Lord, around _____; bestow glory on _____ and lift up his(her) head. ~Amen

Psalm 23:1-3	Lord God, I pray that _____ would be able to say that You are his(her) shepherd, may he(she) not be in want. Lead _____ beside quiet waters, restore his(her) soul; guide _____ in paths of righteousness, for Your name's sake. ~Amen
Psalm 29:11	Dear God, I pray that You would give _____ strength, bless him(her) with peace. ~Amen
Psalm 40:11	Lord, I pray that You will not withhold Your compassion from _____; that Your loving-kindness and Your truth will continually preserve _____. ~Amen
Psalm 119:30	Dear God, cause _____ to choose the way of truth, and may he(she) set his(her) heart on Your laws. ~Amen
Psalm 139:5, 10	Gracious God, I ask that You would go before _____. Please place Your hand of blessing on his(her) head. ~Amen (NLT)
Proverbs 3:5-6	May _____ trust in You, Lord, with all of his(her) heart, don't let him(her) depend on his(her) own understanding. May _____ seek Your will in all he(she) does, please direct his(her) paths. ~Amen (NLT)
Proverbs 6:20-23	Dear God, may _____ obey his(her) father's commands, and not neglect his(her) mother's instruction. May _____ keep our words always in his(her) heart, and tie them around his(her) neck. When he(she) walks, let our counsel guide him(her); when he(she) sleeps, may our words protect him(her); when he(she) wakes up, may our words advise him(her). May _____ see our commands as a lamp, our instruction as a light, and our corrective discipline as a way to life. ~Amen (NLT)

Proverbs 9:10-12   Cause _____ to fear You, Lord, because that is the beginning of wisdom. Fill _____ with knowledge of the Holy One, that results in understanding. May wisdom multiply _____'s days and add years to his(her) life. ~Amen (NLT)

Proverbs 16:20   Lord, I pray that _____ would give heed to Your instruction and prosper; I ask that You bless _____ when he(she) trusts in You, Lord. ~Amen

Isaiah 11:5   Father, may righteousness be _____'s belt, and faithfulness the sash around _____'s waist. ~Amen

Zephaniah 3:17   May _____ know that You, Lord God, is with him(her) and that You are mighty to save. You take great delight in _____, I ask that You quiet _____ with Your love, and rejoice over him(her) with singing. ~Amen

Romans 15:13   I pray that You, the God of hope, would fill _____ with all joy and peace as he(she) trusts in You, so that _____ may overflow with hope by the power of the Holy Spirit. ~Amen

Galatians 5:22-23   God, I ask that You remove the unpleasant things in _____'s heart and fill his(her) heart instead with the fruits of Your Spirit: fill _____ with love and joy and peace, fill _____ with patience and kindness and goodness, fill _____ with gentleness, self-control, and above all else, fill _____ with love. ~Amen

Philippians 4:6-7   Lord, I ask that You not let _____ be anxious about anything, but in everything, through prayer and petition, with thanksgiving, let _____ remember to present their requests to You. And may Your peace, which transcends all understanding, guard _____'s heart and mind in Christ Jesus. ~Amen

2 Thessalonians 1:11-12	Heavenly Father, fulfill every good purpose in _____'s life and every act prompted by his(her) faith, I pray this so that the name of our Lord Jesus Christ may be glorified in _____'s life. ~Amen
James 3:13-16	Heavenly Father, I pray that _____ would be wise and understand Your ways, God; bless him(her) with a life of steady goodness so that his(her) good deeds will pour forth. Don't let _____ become bitterly jealous, or have selfish ambition in his(her) heart, or brag about being wise. Give _____ wisdom that comes from heaven, may he(she) be peace loving, gentle at all times, and willing to yield to others. ~Amen (NLT)

Character

Come into agreement with God that your child's character will reflect the will and glory of God.

Psalm 11:7

Dear Lord, just as You are righteous, I pray that _____ would long to be righteous. Just as You love justice, I pray that _____ would love justice and fight for it. ~Amen

Psalm 13:5-6

Gracious God, help _____ to trust in Your unfailing love, cause _____'s heart to rejoice in Your salvation. May _____ sing to You, Lord, remind _____ of the ways You have been good to him(her). ~Amen

Psalm 25:21

May integrity and uprightness protect _____, may his(her) hope be in You. ~Amen

Psalm 26:2-3

Gracious God, I ask that You would test, _____, O Lord, and try _____, examine his(her) heart and mind; with Your love ever before _____, may he(she) continually walk in Your truth. ~Amen

Psalm 33:20-22

May _____'s soul wait for You, Lord; You are _____'s help and shield. May _____'s heart be glad in You and trust in Your holy name. May Your steadfast love, O Lord, be upon _____, help him(her) hope in You. ~Amen (ESV)

Psalm 34:13-14

Heavenly Father, help _____ to watch his(her) tongue! Keep his(her) lips from telling lies! Help _____ turn away from evil and do good. May he(she) work hard at living in peace with others. ~Amen (NLT)

Psalm 90:14	I pray heavenly Father, that _____ would be satisfied in the morning, with Your steadfast love. May he(she) rejoice and be glad all of his(her) days. ~Amen (ESV)
Psalm 119:9-11	Lord, help _____ ponder how a young person can keep his(her) ways pure. Cause _____ to live according to Your Word, may _____ seek You with all his(her) heart; don't let _____ stray from Your commands, but instead hide Your Word in his(her) heart so that he(she) may not sin against You. ~Amen
Psalm 139:4, 12	Holy Father, You know what _____ is going to say even before he(she) says it. Shine Your light on the darkness of _____'s life so he(she) cannot hide from You. Search _____ and know his(her) heart...lead him(her) in the path of everlasting life. ~Amen
Psalm 141:3-4	Gracious God, At the right times, Lord, would You take control of what _____ says, and keep his(her) lips sealed. May _____ look to You for help, O Sovereign Lord, and be _____'s refuge. ~Amen (NLT)
Proverbs 1:3	Dear God, I pray that _____ would live a disciplined and prudent life, help him(her) do what is right and just and fair. ~Amen
Proverbs 3:3	Lord, I pray that _____ will not let kindness and truth leave him(her), but that _____ would bind them around his(her) neck and write them on the tablet of his(her) heart ~Amen (NASB)
Proverbs 3:7-8	Heavenly Father, keep _____ from being impressed with his(her) own wisdom. Instead, may _____ fear You, Lord, and turn his(her) back on evil so that he(she) will gain renewed health and vitality. ~Amen (NLT)

Proverbs 4:11	Gracious God, I pray that You will guide _____ in the way of wisdom and lead _____ along straight paths. ~Amen
Proverbs 4:5-7	Lord God, may _____ pursue wisdom, and not turn his(her) back on it. May _____ develop good judgment and not forget Your words God. May _____ prize wisdom and realize it's value. ~Amen (NLT)
Proverbs 6:9-11	O God, some days I wonder how long _____ will laze around doing nothing, how long until he(she) gets out of bed. I pray that You show _____ that a nap here, a nap there, a day off here, a day off there can lead to a dirt-poor life, with poverty as his(her) permanent house guest. ~Amen (MSG)
Proverbs 12:19-20	Holy Father, may _____ use truthful words so that they stand the test of time; expose any lies told by _____. May _____ have a heart filled with joy and peace instead of a deceitful heart. ~Amen (NLT)
Proverbs 13:1	Gracious God, I pray that _____ would be a wise child and accept his(her) parent's discipline, don't let _____ refuse to listen to correction. ~Amen (NLT)
Proverbs 19:11	Heavenly Father, I pray that _____ would understand that a person's wisdom gives him(her) patience; may _____ see that it is to his(her) glory to overlook an offense. ~Amen
Proverbs 30:8	Gracious God, would You remove far from _____ falsehood and lying. ~Amen (ESV)

Proverbs 31:25, 30	Lord God, may _____ be clothed with strength and dignity, help him(her) laugh with no fear of the future. Remind _____ that charm is deceptive, beauty does not last, but the one who fears the Lord will be greatly praised. ~Amen (NLT)
Luke 2:52	Heavenly Father, may _____ grow as Jesus did, in wisdom and stature, and in favor with both God and men. ~Amen
Luke 22:31-32	Heavenly Father, when Satan asks to sift _____ like wheat, I pray, as You do Jesus, that his(her) faith will not fail him(her); please strengthen and build up _____. ~Amen (NLT)
John 15:12	God, help _____ follow Your commandment to love each other the way You have loved him(her), especially his(her) brothers and sisters, give them a loving bond and relationship. ~Amen (NLT)
Romans 12:6-8	Lord, You have given each of us different gifts, help _____ to use the gifts You've given; whether it be ministering, teaching, exhorting/encouraging, may he(she) do it well. If You've gifted _____ to give, may he(she) give liberally; if the gift is leading, may he(she) lead with diligence; if the gift is showing mercy, may he(she) give mercy cheerfully. ~Amen (NLT)
Romans 12:12	Father, my prayer for _____ is that he(she) will be joyful in hope, patient in affliction and faithful in prayer. ~Amen
1 Corinthians 6:12	Dear Lord, help _____ to know that just because something is technically legal doesn't mean it is spiritually appropriate. ~Amen (MSG)

1 Corinthians 16:13	Dear Lord, help _____ to be on guard, to stand firm in his(her) faith, to be a man(woman) of courage, and to be strong. Above all, help _____ do everything out of love. ~Amen (NIV)
1 Corinthians 13:4-7	Just as You are loving Lord, cause _____ to be loving, to be patient and kind. May _____ not be jealous or boastful or proud or rude. May _____ never demand his(her) own way, be irritable, or keep a record when he(she) has been wronged. May _____ never be glad about injustice but rejoice whenever the truth wins out. May _____ both know and give love that never gives up, never loses faith, remains hopeful and endures through every circumstance. ~Amen (NLT)
1 Corinthians 13:5	Dear Lord, may _____'s life be marked by love, love that is not rude or self-seeking; may _____ not easily be angered or keep any record of wrongs. ~Amen
2 Corinthians 9:11	Lord, please enrich _____ in every way so that he(she) can always be generous. Because of his(her) generous spirit may people thank You, God. ~Amen
2 Corinthians 15:16	Heavenly Father, may _____'s life be a fragrance presented by Christ to God; may he(she) be a life-giving perfume to those around him(her). ~Amen (NLT)
Ephesians 4:25	Gracious God, I pray that You would help _____ to put off falsehood, and speak truthfully to his(her) friends, for we are all members of one body. ~Amen
Ephesians 5:4	Lord, would You inspire _____ to put away filthiness and foolish talk, as well as crude joking, which are out of place; instead let _____ be filled with thanksgiving. ~Amen (ESV)

Ephesians 6:18

Dear Lord, I pray _____ would grow into a person that prays hard and long, prays for his(her) brothers, sisters, and fellow believers. Help _____ keep his(her) eyes open and keep each other's spirits up so that no one falls behind or drops out. ~Amen (MSG)

Philippians 1:6

God, You have begun a good work in _____, I pray that You will continue to do Your work in him(her) until it is finally finished. ~Amen (NLT)

Philippians 2:14

Gracious God, in everything _____ does, may he(she) stay away from complaining and arguing. ~Amen (NLT)

Philippians 4:8

Today, Lord, I pray for _____ and the things he(she) thinks about. May _____ focus on whatever is true, whatever is honorable, whatever is just, whatever is pure, whatever is lovely, whatever is commendable, anything of excellence, anything worthy of praise, help _____ to think about these things. ~Amen

Philippians 4:12-13

Dear God, help _____ to be satisfied, to know how to live on almost nothing or with everything. Help him(her) learn to secret of living in every situation, with plenty or little, is to do all things with the help of Christ who strengthens him(her). ~Amen (NLT)

Colossians 1:9-10

God, I ask that You give _____ complete knowledge of Your will, as well as spiritual wisdom and understanding. May the way _____ lives always be honoring and pleasing to You, Lord. May _____'s life produce every kind of good fruit, and may he(she) grow and learn to know You better and better, God. ~Amen

Colossians 3:12-14	Dear Lord, would You clothe _____ with tenderhearted mercy, with kindness, with humility, with gentleness, and with patience. May _____ forgive anyone who offends him(her), remembering that You, Lord, forgave him(her). Above all, clothe _____ with love, which binds us all together in perfect harmony. ~Amen
1 Timothy 4:7	Dear God, may _____ not waste time arguing over godless ideas and old wives' tales. Help him(her) spend his(her) time and energy in training himself(herself) for spiritual fitness. ~Amen (NLT)
1 Timothy 6:11	Heavenly Father, may _____ belong to You, God, and run from all things evil. May he(she) follow what is right and good, pursue a godly life, along with faith, love, perseverance, and gentleness. ~Amen (NLT)
2 Timothy 1:7, 9	Lord, I pray that You would give _____ a spirit of power, of love and of self-discipline, keep him(her) from a spirit of timidity; for You have saved _____ and called him(her) to a holy life, by Your purpose and grace, given to _____ in Christ Jesus before the beginning of time. ~Amen
2 Timothy 3:16	Heavenly Father, would You show _____ that all Scripture is inspired by You, God, and is useful to teach what is true. May Your Word make _____ realize what is wrong in his(her) life, may it correct his(her) when he(she) is wrong and may it teach him(her) to do what is right. ~Amen (NLT)

Hebrews 10:25

Heavenly Father, I pray that _____ would not neglect or quit meeting together with other believers, as some teenagers will, instead may he(she) and their friends encourage and warn each other, as we look forward to the day of Your return. ~Amen

Hebrews 12:1

Dear Lord, You have surrounded us with a huge crowd of witnesses to the life of faith; let _____ strip off every weight that slows him(her) down, especially the sin that so easily trips him(her) up. And let _____ run with endurance the race You, God, has set before him(her). ~Amen

James 1:3-5

Heavenly Father, when _____ needs wisdom, remind him(her) to ask You, God, for You will gladly give it and not resent his(her) asking. May _____ fully expect You to answer and not have a doubtful mind that is driven and tossed by the wind. ~Amen (NLT)

2 Peter 1:2-3

God, would You give _____ more and more grace and peace as he(she) grows in knowledge of You. Give _____ everything he(she) needs for living a godly life. ~Amen

2 Peter 1:5-7

Lord, may _____ make every effort to respond to Your promises. Supplement his(her) faith with a generous provision of moral excellence; along with moral excellence, give _____ knowledge, self-control, patient endurance, godliness, brotherly affection and love for everyone. ~Amen (NLT)

1 John 3:7

Gracious God, do not let anyone lead _____ astray. Instead help him(her) to do what is righteous rather than what is sinful. ~Amen

Church

Trust that your prayers about your child's church life are heard by God.

Exodus
20:8

Lord God, remind _____ to observe the Sabbath day by keeping it holy. May he(she) use six days for daily duties and rest on the seventh day, dedicating it to You, Lord ~Amen (NLT)

Matthew
18:20

Heavenly Father, remind _____ of the importance of meeting together with other believers, for where two or more gather together as Christ's followers, You are there among them. ~Amen (NLT)

Faith

Entrust your child to God and know that your prayers are a sweet-smelling offering to the Lord.

Deuteronomy 31:6

O God, I pray that _____ would be strong and take courage. Don't let him(her) be intimidated; don't let him(her) even give it a second thought because You, O God, are striding ahead of _____. You are right there with _____, remind him(her) You won't let him(her) down, You won't leave him(her). ~Amen (MSG)

2 Chronicles 29:11-13

Gracious God, may _____ praise You, Lord, as the glorious God, the majestic God, as his(her) God who displays Your splendor both in heaven and on earth. Remind _____ that all things come from You (wealth and honor, talent and ability). May he(she) give thanks to You and praise Your name. ~Amen

2 Corinthians 10:4-5

Lord God, remind _____ to use Your mighty weapons, God, not mere worldly weapons, to knock down the Devil's strongholds. May _____ use these weapons to break down every proud argument that keeps people from knowing You, God. With these weapons help _____ conquer others rebellious ideas and help he(she) teach others to obey Christ. ~Amen (NLT)

Philippians 3:8-9

Holy Father, I pray that _____ would consider everything else worthless as compared with the infinite value of knowing Christ Jesus as his(her) Lord. For Christ's sake, may _____ discard everything else, counting it all as garbage, so that he(she) can gain Christ and become one with Him. Help _____ no longer count on his(her) own righteousness through obeying the law but realize he(she) become righteous through faith in Christ. ~Amen (NLT)

1 Thessalonians 2:13	Heavenly Father, I pray that when _____ receives the Word of God, he(she) will accept it not as the Word of men, but as it actually is, the Word of God, which is at work in those who believe. ~Amen
1 Timothy 1:5-6	Heavenly Father, cause _____ to listen to Your instruction and be filled with love that comes from a pure heart, a clear conscience, and sincere faith. May _____ not turn away from these things and spend their time arguing and talking foolishness. ~Amen (NLT)
1 Timothy 6:20-21	May _____ guard what You, dear God, have entrusted to him(her). Help _____ avoid godless, foolish discussion with those who oppose You with their so-called knowledge. Don't let _____ wander from the faith by following such foolishness. ~Amen (NLT)
1 Peter 3:15	Heavenly Father, I pray that _____ would always be prepared to give an answer to everyone who asks him(her) to give the reason for the hope he(she) has, and cause _____ to speak with gentleness and with respect. ~Amen
2 Peter 3:18	Gracious God, I pray that _____ would grow in the grace and knowledge of his(her) Lord and Savior Jesus Christ. To You, O God, be glory both now and forever! ~Amen
1 John 3:18	Heavenly Father, I pray that _____ will love not just with words or tongue, but with actions and in truth. ~Amen

Faithful Living

When you pray and show your child the way they should walk with God, they will not depart from it.

Deuteronomy 6:2
Heavenly Father, may _____ and his(her) children fear You as Lord God as long as he(she) lives. Help _____ keep Your decrees and commands so that he(she) may enjoy long life. ~Amen

1 Chronicles 28:9
Heavenly Father, I pray that _____ acknowledges You, Father God, and serve You with wholehearted devotion, and with a willing mind. Remind _____ that You search every heart and understand every motive behind his(her) thoughts. May _____ seek You, for Your Word says, then he(she) will be found by You. ~Amen

Psalm 11:7
Dear Lord, just as You are righteous, I pray that _____ would long to be righteous. Just as You love justice, I pray that _____ would love justice and fight for it. ~Amen

Psalm 16:7, 11
Heavenly Father, may _____ praise You, Lord, as You counsel him(her). Because You are at _____'s right hand he(she) will not be shaken. ~ Amen

Psalm 25:4-5
Gracious God, I pray that You would show _____ the path where he(she) should walk, O Lord, point out the right road for him(her) to follow. Lead _____ by Your truth and teach him(her), for You are the God who saves _____. All day long, may he(she) put his(her) hope in You. ~Amen (NLT)

Psalm 25:14-15	Lord, You promise to be a friend to those who fear You. Be _____'s friend and teach him(her) about Your covenant. Help _____ keep his(her) eyes on You, rescue him(her) from the traps of the enemy. ~Amen
Psalm 37:1-7	May _____ trust in You, Lord and do good. May _____ delight himself(herself) in You. May _____ commit his(her) ways to You, Lord, and trust in You. May _____ be still and know that You are the Lord, and that You wait patiently for him(her). Lord, would You give _____ the desires of his(her) heart. ~Amen
Psalm 37:4-5	Cause _____ to delight in You, Lord. Would You bless him(her) with the desires of his(her) heart. Let _____ commit everything he(she) does to You, and trust in You, because You will help him(her). ~Amen (NLT)
Psalm 55:22	Dear Lord, help _____ cast all his(her) cares on You, Lord, and remind _____ that You will sustain him(her), You will never let the righteous fall. ~Amen
Psalm 130: 3-5	Lord, if You kept a record of our sins, who, O Lord, could ever survive? Remind _____ that You offer forgiveness, help him(her) learn to fear You and learn to count on You, Lord. May _____ put his(her) hope in Your Word. ~Amen (NLT)
Proverbs 24:5-6	Lord, give _____ wisdom in all things because the wise are mightier than the strong, and those with knowledge grow stronger and stronger. May _____ seek wise guidance since victory depends on having advisers. ~Amen

Amos 5:14

Dear Lord, I pray that _____ would seek good, not evil, so that he(she) may live; Lord God Almighty, I ask that you be with _____. ~Amen

Micah 6:8

May _____ realize what You, Lord, require of a person: Help _____ to act justly, and to love mercy, and to walk humbly with You, God. ~Amen

Matthew 5:6

Dear God, would You bless _____ and cause him(her) to hunger and thirst for righteousness, for You have promised to fill those who hunger for You. ~Amen

Matthew 5:7

Dear Lord, I pray that You would bless _____ with a merciful spirit, a merciful heart, for You have promised to show him(her) mercy. ~Amen

Matthew 17:20

Dear Lord, I pray You would give _____ faith the size of a mustard seed; when he(she) tells this mountain "Move from here to there," it will move. Help _____ realize that nothing will be impossible for You. ~Amen (HCSB)

Acts 19:20

Gracious God, I pray that Your message will move in _____'s life and have a powerful effect. ~Amen

1 Corinthians 2:9 & Isaiah 64:4

Thank You, God, for the Scriptures, in them You tell us: No eye has seen, no ear has heard, and no mind has imagined what You have prepared for _____ because You love him(her). Help _____ be willing to wait for You to work on his(her) behalf. ~Amen (NLT)

1 Corinthians 15:58

Dear God, I pray during _____'s life, he(she) would be strong and immovable, always working enthusiastically for You Lord, knowing that nothing he(she) does for You is ever useless. ~Amen (NLT)

Ephesians
3:16-17a

I pray that out of Your glorious riches, Lord, You would strengthen _____ with power through Your Spirit in his(her) inner being, so that Christ may dwell in _____'s heart through faith. ~Amen

Philippians
2:15-16

Dear God, may _____ live a clean, innocent life as Your child, God, in this dark world full of crooked and perverse people. Let _____'s life shine brightly before others, and hold tightly to the Word of life. ~Amen (NLT)

Titus
3:4-5

God, You are the Savior, I pray that You would show _____ Your kindness and Your love. Save _____, not because of anything he(she) has done but because of Your mercy. Wash away _____'s sins and give him(her) new life through the Holy Spirit. ~Amen (NLT)

1 Peter
2:11-12

Dear Lord, I pray that You help _____ remember this world is not his(her) home and not let him(her) self get too cozy in it, indulging his(her) ego at the sake of his(her) soul. May _____ live an exemplary life so that his(her) actions will win others over to God's side and be there to join in the celebration when Christ arrives. ~Amen (MSG)

1 John
3:1

Dear Lord, remind _____ how great is the love You have lavished on him(her), _____ is called a child of God, and that is what _____ is: Your child. ~Amen

1 John
5:14

Gracious God, I pray that You would give _____ confidence as he(she) approaches You; help him(her) know that if he(she) asks anything according to Your will, You hear. ~Amen

Family

God cares about your family relationships. Trust God with them.

Psalm
133:1   Lord, help each one in our family make our home a wonderful and pleasant place where brothers (and sisters) live together in harmony! ~Amen (NLT)

Romans
12:10   Lord, I pray that _____ and his(her) siblings would love each other with genuine affection, and take delight in honoring each other. ~Amen (NLT)

Romans
14:19   Dear God, I pray that my children would use all his(her) energy in getting along with each other; help them choose encouraging words and not drag each other down by finding fault. ~Amen (MSG)

Romans
15:5, 7   Faithful God, would You give _____ patience and encouragement; help him(her) live in complete harmony with his(her) siblings, as is fitting for followers of Christ Jesus. Help _____ to accept others just as Christ has accepted him(her), so that You, God, will be given glory. ~Amen

Ephesians
4:32   Gracious God, show _____ and his(her) siblings how to be kind and compassionate to one another, forgiving each other, just as You have forgiven each of them. ~Amen

Colossians
2:2   Lord God, may _____ and his(her) siblings be knit together by strong ties of love.   Give _____ full confidence and complete understanding of Your plan, and of Christ. ~Amen

2 Thessalonians 3:16

As a parent, God, I ask that You, the Lord of peace himself, bring me peace at all times, in every way. I know that You are with me, and with my children. ~Amen (ESV)

2 Timothy 2:24-26

Heavenly Father, do not permit _____ to be quarrelsome; instead, cause him(her) to be gentle, patient, and humble, especially when his(her) siblings are in the wrong...because then they will be more likely, with God's help, to turn away from their wrong ideas and believe what is true. ~Amen

1 Peter 3:8-9a

Lord God, I pray that You would help _____ live in harmony with his(her) siblings, help _____ be sympathetic, compassionate, and humble. Don't let _____ and his(her) sibling(s) repay evil with evil or insult with insult, but with blessing. ~Amen

Friendship

Pray for your child to have the kind of friendships that glorify God.

**Psalm
101:6**

Heavenly Father, give _____ faithful people to be his(her) companions. ~Amen (NLT)

**Ecclesiastes
4:9, 12**

Heavenly Father, would You bless _____ with friends who will reach out and help when he(she) falls; friends who can stand back to back and together conquer when attacked. ~Amen (NLT)

**Proverbs
11:13**

Lord, I pray that _____ would not gossip, because gossip betrays a confidence, but that _____ would be a trustworthy person who is able to keep a confidence. ~Amen

**Proverbs
12:17**

Heavenly Father, help _____ be an honest witness who tells the truth. Help him(her) not be a person who makes cutting remarks, instead give him(her) words of wisdom that bring healing. ~Amen

**Proverbs
12:18 and
18:21**

Gracious God, remind _____ that reckless words pierce like a sword, but the tongue of the wise brings healing. Also, remind _____ that the tongue has the power of life and death. ~Amen

**Proverbs
12:26 and
1 Corinthians
15:33**

Dear God, I pray that _____ would give good advice to his(her) friends. Remind _____ that bad company corrupts good morals. ~Amen (NLT)

Proverbs 17:17, 18:24	Dear God, as iron sharpens iron, surround _____ with friends that will sharpen him(her) as a friend. May _____ be a real friend that sticks closer than a brother. ~Amen
Proverbs 20:3	Heavenly Father, help _____ not be a fool who is quick to quarrel, remind him(her) that it is to a person's honor to avoid strife. ~Amen
Proverbs 22:24-25	Dear Lord, help _____ not befriend angry people or associate with hot-tempered people, keep him(her) from learning to be like them and endangering his(her) own soul. ~Amen (NLT)
Matthew 5:41	Gracious God, grow _____ into the kind of person who, if asked to go a mile for someone, will go two miles. ~Amen
Matthew 5:44	Heavenly Father, may _____ be the kind of person who loves his(her) enemies and prays for those who persecute him(her), please show that he(she) is a son(daughter) of heaven. ~Amen
Luke 6:36-38	Loving God, I pray that _____ would be merciful, just as You, his(her) Father is merciful. Help _____ not to be judgmental or condemning but forgiving. May _____ be giving -- a good measure, pressed down, shaken together, running over and poured into his(her) lap. Remind _____ that with the measure he(she) uses, that same measure will be used with him(her). ~Amen

2 Corinthians 1:4 Heavenly Father, I ask that You would comfort _____ in all of his(her) troubles, so that he(she) can comfort others when they are troubled, with the same comfort You have given him(her). ~Amen (NLT)

Ephesians 4:29 Gracious Father, do not let any unwholesome talk come out of _____'s mouth, but only what is helpful for building others up according to their needs, that it may benefit those who listen. ~Amen

Philippians 1:4-7 Holy Father, give _____ a friend, a partner with whom he(she) can spread the Good News about Christ with. May they pray for each other, and have a special place in their hearts for each other. ~Amen (NLT)

1 Thessalonians 5:15 Dear Lord, I pray _____ would develop into a patient person, attentive to individual needs. When others get on his(her) nerves, may ____ be careful not to snap at them but to look for the best in each other, and bring out the best in them. ~Amen (MSG)

1 Timothy 4:12-13 Heavenly Father, help _____ to be like Timothy and be an Christian example to those around him(her) in the way he(she) lives, in the way he(she) loves, by his(her) faith and purity. May _____ focus on reading the Scriptures, encouraging fellow believers and teaching them. ~Amen (NLT)

Titus 2:1-2 Dear God, surround _____ with people whose lives reflect wholesome teaching, with people who exercise self-control, are worthy of respect, and those that live wisely. Let him(her) witness those that have a sound faith and are filled with love and patience. ~Amen (NLT)

James 4:4   Heavenly Father, let _____ seek friendship with You rather than with the world, remembering that anyone who chooses to be a friend of the world becomes Your enemy. ~Amen

Future

You can trust the God has a hope and a good future for your child; pray for that future to be fulfilled.

Genesis 29:20
Heavenly Father, I pray that _____ would be like Jacob: willing to wait for Your perfect timing in finding a spouse, and may that time pass quickly, as it did for Jacob. ~Amen (NLT)

2 Samuel 22:31
Dear Lord, Show _____ that Your way, God, is perfect, that Your Word is proven. Be _____'s shield as he(she) trusts in You. ~Amen (NLT)

Job 1:10
Lord, I pray that You would protect _____, his(her) home and his(her) property from all harm. Bless _____ and make him(her) prosperous in everything he(she) does. ~Amen (NLT)

Psalm 61:6-7
Dear Lord, I pray that You would add many years to _____'s life; may Your unfailing love and faithfulness watch over him(her).~Amen (NLT)

Psalm 90:12
Gracious God, Teach _____ to make the most of his(her) time, help him(her) grow in wisdom. ~Amen (NLT)

Psalm 119:105
Dear Lord, I pray that Your Word would be a lamp to _____'s feet and a light for his(her) path. ~Amen (ESV)

Psalm 138:8
Lord, I pray and ask that You would fulfill Your purpose for _____; may he(she) know that Your steadfast love endures forever. ~Amen (ESV)

Proverbs 3:4	Gracious God, I pray that _____ will win favor and a good name in the sight of You, God, and of men. ~Amen
Proverbs 16:3	Gracious God, help _____ commit to the Lord whatever he(she) does so that _____'s plans will succeed. ~Amen
Proverbs 19:21	Heavenly Father, no matter what _____ is planning in his(her) heart, let Your purpose prevail in _____'s life. ~Amen
Proverbs 22:29	Gracious God, teach _____ to be a person skilled in their work, so that he(she) may serve before kings. ~Amen (Proverbs 22:29 NLT)
Isaiah 48:17	Lord God, I pray that You would be _____'s Lord and God, be the one who teaches him(her) what is good; please lead _____ on the only path he(she) should follow. ~Amen (NLT)
Jeremiah 10:23	Gracious God, May_____ realize that his(her) life is not his(her) own, may _____ look to You to direct his(her) steps. ~Amen
Jeremiah 29:11-13	You know, O Lord, the plans You have for _____, plans for good and not for disaster, to give him(her) a future and a hope. May _____ pray to You, and listen for You, may he(she) look for You, God, in earnest; You have promised to find _____ when he(she) seeks You. ~Amen (NLT)
Matthew 26:41	Lord God, when _____ is yearning for a dating relationship, help him(her) to stay alert and pray, so that temptation will not overpower him(her). Strengthen _____'s spirit when his(her) body is weak. ~Amen (NLT)

Romans 12:6-8

Lord, You have given each of us different gifts, help _____ to use the gifts You've given; whether it be ministering, teaching, exhorting/encouraging, may he(she) do it well. If You've gifted _____ to give, may he(she) give liberally; if the gift is leading, may he(she) lead with diligence; if the gift is showing mercy, may he(she) give mercy cheerfully. ~Amen. (NLT)

2 Corinthians 6:14-17

Dear God, when _____ dates, may he(she) not team up with those who are unbelievers. May _____ see that goodness cannot partner with wickedness, and light cannot live with darkness. Remind _____ that he(she) is a temple of the living God. ~Amen (NLT)

Philippians 3:13-14

Dear Lord, I pray that _____ would forget the past and look forward to what lies ahead, help him(her) press on to reach the end of the race and receive the heavenly prize for which God, through Christ Jesus, is calling him(her). ~Amen (NLT)

1 Peter 5:7-8a

Dear Lord, as _____ drives, help him(her) cast all his(her) anxieties on You, because You are for _____. Help _____ to be self-controlled and alert when he's(she)'s behind the wheel. And for me Lord, help me cast my anxieties on You when _____ is driving the car. ~Amen

3 John 2

Lord God, I pray that _____ would have good fortune in everything he(she) does. May _____ be in good health, and may his(her) everyday affairs prosper, as well as his(her) soul. ~Amen (MSG)

Heart

Pray for God to touch, heal, and protect your child's heart.

1 Kings 16:7-11 Gracious God, I pray that You would give _____ a wise and discerning heart so that he(she) can distinguish between right and wrong. ~Amen

1 Chronicles 29:17-18 Remind _____, dear Lord, that You examine his(her) heart and You will rejoice when You find integrity there. I pray that all that _____'s does would be done with good motive. Help _____ want to obey You; may his(her) love for You never change. ~Amen (NLT)

2 Chronicles 28:9 Heavenly Father, I pray that _____ acknowledge You, Father God, and serve You with wholehearted devotion, and with a willing mind. Remind _____ that You search every heart and understand every motive behind his(her) thoughts. May _____ seek You, for Your Word says, then he(she) will be found by You. ~Amen

Ezra 7:10 Dear God, May _____ be like Ezra, and set his(her) heart to study the Law of the Lord, and to do it, and to teach it. ~Amen (ESV)

Psalm 51:17 Dear Lord, Show _____ that the sacrifice You want, O God, is a broken spirit; a broken and repentant heart You will not despise. ~Amen (NLT)

Psalm 86:11 Gracious God, I pray that You would teach _____ Your way, O Lord, and help _____ walk in Your truth; give _____ an undivided heart that he(she) may fear Your name. ~Amen

Proverbs 14:30	Gracious God, May _____ have a tranquil heart, which gives life to the flesh; and not envy, which makes the bones rot. ~Amen (ESV)
Jeremiah 49:16	Loving God, ever so gently, would You help _____ understand that the pride of his(her) heart has deceived him(her). ~Amen.
Ezekiel 11:19-20	Lord, I pray that You would give _____ singleness of heart and a put a new spirit within him(her). May You take away _____'s stony, stubborn heart and give him(her) a tender, responsive heart; help him(her) obey Your decrees and regulations and be _____'s God. ~Amen (NLT)
Matthew 5:8	Dear God, bless _____ and give him(her) a pure heart; for those pure in heart will see You. ~Amen
Matthew 5:9	Dear Lord, bless _____ with the heart of a peacemaker, for the peacemakers will be called sons of God. ~Amen
John 13:34-35	Dear Lord, I pray that _____ would love others in the same way that You love people. Help his(her) friends to see _____'s compassion to others and know that he(she) is Your disciple. ~Amen

Life Issues

Life might get hard sometimes, but you can bring your worries before God's throne.

2 Samuel 22:31	Dear Lord, Show _____ that Your way, God, is perfect, that Your Word is proven. Be _____'s shield as he(she) trusts in You. ~Amen (NLT)
Psalm 18:1-2	Lord, I ask that You would be _____'s strength when he(she) drives. Be _____'s rock; form a fortress around him(her) as he(she) travels. Be _____'s deliverer when danger approaches and provide Your shield and horn when _____ is not even aware that he(she) needs protection. Be the stronghold in _____'s life and grant traveling mercies upon him(her). ~Amen
Proverbs 2:1-3	Lord, may _____ listen to what You say and treasure Your commands. When he(she) tunes into music, tune his(her) ear to wisdom, help him(her) concentrate on the lyrics and cry out for insight and ask for understanding as to music choices. ~Amen (NLT)
Proverbs 5:21-23	Dear Lord, convict _____'s heart and remind him(her) that his(her) ways are in full view of You, Lord, and that You examine all his(her) paths, especially when it comes to screen time. I pray that the evilness there will not ensnare _____, that the cords of sin will not hold him(her) fast. Build discipline into _____'s character so that he(she) will not be led astray. ~Amen

Proverbs 13:11, 23:4

Dear God, help _____ understand that the one who gathers money little by little makes it grow. Help _____ not to wear himself(herself) out trying to get rich; instead grow in _____ self-control so that he(she) can restrain himself(herself). ~Amen

Philippians 4:19 & 1 Chronicles 29:14

Dear Lord, remind _____ that everything he(she) has comes from You, and that You, the God who cares for _____, will supply all of his(her) needs from Your glorious riches, which have been given to us in Christ. ~Amen (NLT)

Hebrews 13:5 & Philippians 4:12

Heavenly Father, keep _____'s life free from the love of money and let him(her) be content with what he(she) has, knowing that You, O Lord, will never leave him(her) or forsake him(her). Let _____ be like Paul, who knew how to be content in any and every situation, whether well fed or hungry, whether living in plenty or in want. ~Amen

1 Timothy 3:8-9

Gracious God, may _____ have strong faith. May he(she) be respected and have integrity. May he(she) not be a heavy drinker or greedy for money but instead be committed to reveal truths of the Christian faith and live with a clear conscience. ~Amen (NLT)

1 Timothy 6:10

Wise God, block _____ from craving money, for the love of money is at the root of all kinds of evil. Don't let him(her) wander from the faith and pierce him(herself) with many sorrows because he(she) seeks to have money. ~Amen (NLT)

1 Timothy 6:18

Gracious God, I pray that _____ would learn to use his(her) money to do good. May he(she) be rich in good works and generous to those in need, always ready to share with others. ~Amen (NLT)

Love God's Word

Pray for your child to love God's Word and to enjoy reading and learning about His love for them.

Deuteronomy 6:4-5

Heavenly Father, may _____ love You, Lord God, with all his(her) heart, love You with all his(her) soul and love You with all his(her) strength. ~Amen

Psalm 1:1-3

Gracious God, I pray that _____ would take delight in Your law, let him(her) meditate on it day and night, so that whatever he(she) does will prosper. ~Amen

Psalm 19:7-9

Lord God, May _____ know the law of the Lord, may it revive his(her) soul. May _____ trust in the decrees of the Lord and gain wisdom. May _____ follow the commandments of the Lord, which are right and bring joy to the heart. May _____ obey the commands of the Lord which are clear and give insight to life. May _____ revere You, Lord, out of a pure heart. ~Amen (NLT)

Psalm 19:10

Dear God, I pray that _____ would discover that Your Word is better than a diamond, better than a diamond set between emeralds. May he(she) like it better than red, ripe strawberries in the spring. ~Amen (MSG)

Psalm 27:8-9

Lord, when _____'s heart hears You say, "Come and talk to me," may his(her) heart respond, "Lord, I am coming." ~Amen (NLT)

Psalm 33:4

Lord, I pray that _____ will know that Your Word is right and true, and that he(she) can know You are faithful in all You do.~Amen (NLT)

Nahum 1:7

Heavenly Father, help _____ know that You are good, that You are a refuge in times of trouble, for You care for those who trust You. ~Amen

Luke 24:45

Lord God, I pray that You would open _____'s mind so that he(she) can understand the Scriptures. ~Amen

John 8:31

Dear God, may _____ abide in the Word and know the truth, because the truth will set them free. ~Amen (ESV)

John 14:21

Heavenly Father, cause _____ to know Your commands and obey them out of his(her) love for You. Thank You for loving _____, Father. ~Amen (NLT)

Acts 17:11

Gracious God, may _____ be like a Berean and listen eagerly to the messages in church. Prompt _____ to search the Scriptures day after day to check up on the pastor's teaching, and see if they are teaching the truth. ~Amen (NLT)

Philippians 1:9-11

Wonderful Father, this is my prayer: that _____'s love may abound more and more in knowledge and depth of insight, may _____ be able to discern what is best and may he(she) be pure and blameless until the day of Christ, I pray that _____ will be filled with the fruit of righteousness that comes through Jesus Christ -- to the glory and praise of God. ~Amen

Colossians **2:7-8**	Heavenly Father, let _____'s roots grow down into You, Lord, and draw up nourishment from Christ, so he(she) will grow in faith, strong and vigorous in the truth. Let _____'s life overflow with thanksgiving for all he(she) done. ~Amen (NLT)
Colossians **3:17**	Gracious God, whatever _____ does, in word or deed, let him(her) do everything in the name of Jesus, giving thanks to You. ~Amen
1 Peter **2:2**	Heavenly Father, may _____ be like a newborn baby, who craves the pure spiritual milk so that it will nourish his(her) soul and help him(her) grow up in his(her) salvation. ~Amen

Mind and Body

God will hear your prayers for your child's mind and body. Trust that He welcomes you to His throne room in prayer.

1 Samuel 16:7

Gracious God, I pray that You would remind _____ that You see him(her) through Your eyes; You don't see his(her) appearance, You see _____'s heart. ~Amen

Matthew 5:34, 37

Dear Lord, help _____ to not swear at all. Let his(her) "Yes" simply be "Yes" and his(her) "No" simply be "No." ~Amen

1 Corinthians 6:19-20

Gracious God, Remind _____ that his(her) body is a temple of the Holy Spirit, which is in him(her). Remind _____ that he(she) is not his(her) own, that You bought him(her) with a price. May _____ honor You with his(her) body. ~Amen

Ephesians 2:10

Dear God, remind _____ that he(she) is Your workmanship, created in Christ Jesus to do good works, works which You have prepared in advance for _____ to do. ~Amen (NLT)

Ephesians 3:17-19

Father, I pray that _____'s identity will be firmly rooted and established in Christ's love, and that _____ may have power, together with all the saints, to grasp how wide and long and high and deep is the love of Christ, and to know this love that surpasses knowledge--that he(she)may be filled to the measure of all the fullness of God. ~Amen

Colossians 3:17

Gracious God, Whatever _____ does, in word or deed, let him(her) do everything in the name of Jesus, giving thanks to You. ~Amen

1 Timothy 2:9	Glorious God, may _____ be modest in his(her) appearance. Remind him(her) to wear decent and appropriate clothing so he(she) won't draw attention to himself(herself) or cause others to stumble into sin when they look at him(her). ~Amen (NLT)
Hebrews 11:6	Holy Father, I pray that _____ would understand it is impossible to please You apart from faith. May he(she) come to You and believe that You exist and know that You reward those who sincerely seek You. ~Amen (NLT)
1 Peter 3:3-4	Dear Lord, help _____ not be concerned about the outward beauty of fancy hairstyles, expensive jewelry, or beautiful clothes. Instead, may he(she) clothe him(her)self with the beauty that comes from within, the unfading beauty of a gentle and quiet spirit, which is so precious to God. ~Amen (NLT)
1 Peter 5:8-9	Heavenly Father, make _____ self-controlled and alert. Remind him(her) that our enemy the devils prowls around like a roaring lion looking for someone to devour. Help _____ to resist him and to stand firm in the faith. ~Amen

Missions

When you pray the words of Scripture, you are praying God's heart. Trust that God will help your child share His love.

Daniel 5:21

Heavenly Father, help _____ learn that You, the Most High God who rules over the kingdoms of the world and appoints anyone He desires to rule over them, that authorities in his(her) life have been put there by You, God. ~Amen (NLT)

Psalm 89:1

Heavenly Father, let _____ sing of Your love forever; let _____ make known Your faithfulness through all generations. ~Amen

Proverbs 31:20

Heavenly Father, I pray that _____ would open his(her) arms to the poor and extend his(her) hands to the needy. ~Amen

Matthew 4:19 NLT

Holy Father, give _____ the desire to follow after You, Jesus, and make _____ a fisher of people. ~Amen (NLT)

Matthew 5:11-12

Heavenly Father, bless _____ when he(she) is insulted or persecuted, or when others falsely say all kinds of evil against him(her) because of Christ. May _____ rejoice and be glad because his(her) reward is in heaven. ~Amen

Matthew 5:13-14

God, bless _____ help him(her) be the salt of the earth, a light to the world, a city on a hill that cannot be hidden. ~Amen

Matthew 5:16

Gracious God, may _____'s good deeds shine out for all to see, so that everyone will praise You, Heavenly Father. ~Amen (NLT)

**Matthew
28:19-20**

Heavenly Father, I pray that _____ would go and make disciples of all nations, baptizing them in the name of the Father and the Son and the Holy Spirit. Help _____ teach these new disciples to obey all of Your commands; remind _____ that You are always with him(her), even to the end of the age. ~Amen (NLT)

**Romans
1:16 NLT**

Dear Lord, may _____ not be ashamed of the Good News about Christ but know that it is the power of God at work, saving everyone who believes. ~Amen (NLT)

**Romans
12:13**

Heavenly Father, I pray that _____ would share with God's people who are in need, may he(she) be always ready to help them. And may _____ always be eager to practice hospitality. ~Amen

Others

God calls us to be persistent in prayer. Never give up praying for your child.

Zechariah 7:9

Heavenly Father, may _____ judge fairly, may he(she) show mercy and kindness to others, especially to widows and orphans, foreigners and poor people, those in great need. ~Amen (NLT)

Matthew 25:35-40

Lord God, fill _____ with compassion: when he(she) sees someone who is hungry, may he(she) feed them or give them drink, may _____ be inviting, give clothing, care for the sick, visit those in prison...meet the needs of others and by doing so show the love of Christ. ~Amen (NLT)

Mark 12:30-31

May _____ love You Lord God, with all of his(her) heart, all of his(her) soul, all of his(her) mind, and all of his(her) strength. And let _____ love his(her) neighbor as himself(herself), because there is no commandment greater than these. ~Amen (NLT)

Luke 6:27-31

Holy God, may _____ listen to Your words and do good to those who oppose You, God. May he(she) pray for happiness for all those around him(her). Help _____ give what he(she) has to anyone who asks for it, and do for others what he(she) would like them to do for him(her). ~Amen (NLT)

John 13:34-35

Dear Lord, I pray that _____ would love others in the same way that You love people. Help his(her) friends to see _____'s compassion to others and know that he(she) is Your disciple. ~Amen

2 Corinthians 9:6-8

Lord God, teach _____ to sow generously so that he(she) might reap generously. Guide him(her) in how much he(she) should give. May _____ not give reluctantly or in response to pressure; let him(her) be a person who loves You and gives cheerfully. ~Amen (NLT)

Galatians 6:9-10

Lord God, may _____ not get tired of doing what is good. Remind him(her) that at just the right time he(she) will reap a harvest of blessing if he(she) doesn't give up. Whenever _____ has the opportunity, let him(her) do good to everyone-- especially to those in the family of faith. ~Amen (NLT)

Ephesians 5:15-17

Lord God, cause _____ to be careful how to live, may he(she) not be foolish but wise. Help _____ to make the most of every opportunity to do good to others, and to understand what Your will for him(her) is, Lord. ~Amen (NLT)

Philippians 2:3-4

Lord God, help _____ not be selfish or live to make a good impression on others. Instead let _____ be humble, thinking of others as better than himself(herself). May _____ not think only about his(her) own affairs, but be interested in others too, and what they are doing. ~Amen (NLT)

1 Timothy 2:2

Gracious God, may _____ have a heart to pray for people and ask for You to show mercy to them. May he(she) pray for those in authority in his(her) life (like teachers and coaches) so that we can live in peace and quietness, in godliness and dignity. ~Amen (NLT)

Hebrews **13:2-3**	Gracious God, do not let _____ forget to entertain strangers, for by doing so some have entertained angels without knowing it. ~Amen
James **2:14-17**	Gracious God, let _____ prove his(her) faith by his(her) actions: when he(she) sees those in need of food or clothing (or other things) may _____ live out his(her) faith and help them. ~Amen (NLT)
1 Peter **2:11-12**	Dear Lord, I pray that You help _____ remember this world is not his(her) home and not let him(her)self get too cozy in it, indulging his(her) ego at the sake of his(her) soul. May _____ live an exemplary life so that his(her) actions will win others over to God's side and be there to join in the celebration when Christ arrives. ~Amen (MSG)
1 Peter **2:17**	Gracious God, may _____ have respect for everyone, and love his(her) Christian brothers and sisters. May _____ fear God, and respect those in authority over him(her) (including teachers and coaches). ~Amen (NLT)
1 Peter **4:8-11**	Heavenly Father, above all, may _____ love others deeply, because love covers a multitude of sins. May _____ use whatever gifts he(she) has received to serve others, faithfully administering Your grace in its various forms. May _____ serve with the strength You provide, so that in all things You, O Lord, will be praised and receive and glory. ~Amen
1 Peter **4:10-11**	God, You have given each of us a gift from Your great variety of spiritual gifts; cause _____ to use his(her) gifts well, to serve others. May _____ serve others with strength and energy that You supply God, and bring You glory. ~Amen (NLT)

Parent/Child Relationship

Seek God's wisdom in parenting your child.

Proverbs 1:8-9	Gracious God, I pray that _____ would listen to what his(her) father teaches him(her). May _____ not neglect his(her) mother's teaching. Let _____ see that what he(she) learns from a parent will crown him(her) with grace and clothe him(her) with honor. ~Amen (NLT)
Proverbs 22:6	Heavenly Father, help us to train _____ in the way that he(she) should go, so that when he(she) is old he(she) will not turn from it. ~Amen (Proverbs 22:6)
Ephesians 6:1-3	Dear Lord, cause _____ To obey us as parents, because he(she) belongs to You, Lord, for this is the right thing to do. May _____ honor his(her) father and mother, so that he(she) will live a long life, full of blessing. ~Amen (NLT)
Ephesians 6:4	Lord, as parents, help us not provoke _____ to anger by the way we treat them. Rather, help us bring up_____ with the discipline and instruction that comes from You, Lord. ~Amen (NLT)
Colossians 3:15	Lord, would You help _____ let the peace that comes from Christ rule in his(her)heart. You have called us, may _____ live in peace and always be thankful. ~Amen (NLT)

1 Thessalonians 2:12	Dear God, help me as a parent to encourage, comfort, and urge _____ to live a life worthy of God, who has called him(her) into his kingdom and glory. ~Amen
Hebrews 12:5-10	Father, may _____ recognize that when we, his(her) parents, discipline him(her), it means that we love him(her) and that he(she) belongs to our family, just as You discipline those You love, those You accept as Your sons and daughters. May _____ respect us when we discipline him(her), realizing that we are doing our best and that we ourselves are submitting to Your discipline, which is for our good. ~Amen

Praise

Our praises are a fragrant offering to God. Pray for your child to understand how to praise their creator.

Isaiah 9:6
Gracious God, teach _____ to praise You, God, as we celebrate this day that a child is born to us, a Son has been given to us; the government will rest on His shoulders. May _____ know You as his(her) Wonderful Counselor, the Mighty God, the Everlasting Father, and the Prince of Peace. ~Amen (NLT)

1 Samuel 12:24
Gracious God, may _____ be sure to fear You, Lord, and sincerely worship You. Bring to his(her) mind all the wonderful things You have done for him(her). ~Amen (NLT)

1 Chronicles 16:8-11
Heavenly Father, may _____ give thanks to You, God, and call on Your name. May he(she) sing to You and tell of all Your wonderful acts. May _____ glory in Your holy name; as he(she) seeks You, let him(her) rejoice. May _____ look to You, Lord and to Your strength, may _____ seek Your face always. ~Amen

1 Chronicles 29:11-13
Gracious God, may _____ praise You, Lord, as the glorious God, the majestic God, as his(her) God who displays Your splendor both in heaven and on earth. Remind _____ that all things come from You (wealth and honor, talent and ability). May he(she) give thanks to You and praise Your name. ~Amen (1 Chronicles 29:11-13)

Psalm 5:11

Heavenly Father, may _____ take refuge in You, Lord, and rejoice. May he(she) sing joyful praises forever. Protect _____, Lord, so that he(she) will love Your name and be filled with joy. ~Amen (NLT)

Psalm 100:2-3

Gracious God, may _____ worship You, Lord, with gladness. May he(she) come before You, singing with joy and acknowledge that You are the Lord God. You made ___ and he(she) is one of Yours. ~Amen (NLT)

Psalm 122:1

Heavenly Father, may _____ be like David, who is glad with those that say "Let us go to the house of the Lord." May he(she) love to praise You. ~Amen (NLT)

Prodigal

Pray for your child with fervent prayers when they are a prodigal so they will return to the heart of God.

Isaiah 54:10   Heavenly Father, though the mountains be shaken and the hills be removed, remind _____ of Your unfailing love which will not be shaken. Remind _____ of Your compassion for him(her). ~Amen

Psalm 55:16-18   Gracious God, remind _____ to call on You, God, for You will rescue him(her). Be it morning, noon, or night when _____ is in distress, You, O Lord, hear his(her) voice. Rescue _____ and keep him(her) safe. ~Amen (NLT)

Psalm 63:7-8   Good and Gracious God, remind _____ how much You have helped him(her); may _____ sing for joy in the shadow of Your protecting wings. Follow close behind _____, I praise You that Your right hand holds _____ securely. ~Amen (NLT)

Psalm 90:8, 12   You, O Lord, spread out _____'s sins , his(her) secret sins, and You see them all. When _____ stumbles, teach him(her) to make the most of his(her) time so that he(she) may grow in wisdom. ~Amen (NLT)

Psalm 91

Heavenly Father, let _____ dwell in the shelter of the Most High and rest in the shadow of the Almighty. Be _____'s refuge, his(her) fortress, be _____'s covering, his(her) shield. Do not let him(her) fear the terror of the night, nor any type of plague or sickness. Do not let any harm or disaster come near _____. Command Your angels to guard _____ in all his(her) ways and keep him(her) from hurting himself(herself). When _____ calls on You, answer him(her). Be with _____ in trouble, deliver him(her), and honor him(her). Satisfy _____ with long life and show him(her) Your salvation. ~Amen

Psalm 91:11

Heavenly Father, I pray that You, God, will order Your angels to protect _____ wherever he(she) goes. ~Amen (NLT)

Psalm 121:7-8

Lord, I ask that You would keep all harm from _____ and watch over his(her) life. Keep watch, Lord, over _____ as he(she) comes and goes, both now and forevermore. ~Amen

Psalm 125:2

Lord God, just as the mountains surround and protect Jerusalem, Lord, I pray that You would surround and protect _____, both now and forevermore. ~Amen (NLT)

John 10:4-5

Lord God, I pray that _____ would know Your voice, as his(her) shepherd; may he(she) never follow a stranger, in fact may they run away when then don't recognize the stranger's voice. ~Amen

Protection

God promises His protection over His children. Pray God's words when your child needs protection.

Psalm 17:8-9 Heavenly Father, I pray that You would guard _____ as the apple of Your eye; hide him(her) in the shadow of Your wings. Protect _____ from wicked people who might attack him(her). ~Amen (NLT)

Psalm 18:16 Lord, would You reach down from on high and take hold of _____, draw him(her) out of deep waters. ~Amen

Psalm 121:1, 2, 5 Gracious God, I pray when _____ looks up the mountains, he(she) know that his(her) strength does not come from them but from You, O God, the one who made heaven and earth and mountains. God, You are _____'s guardian, be right at his(her) side, protecting him(her). ~Amen (MSG)

School

Pray for your child their school and the people who teach your child.

2 Chronicles 16:8-11 Heavenly Father, may _____ give thanks to You, God, and call on Your name. May he(she) sing to You and tell of all Your wonderful acts. May _____ glory in Your holy name; as he(she) seeks You, let him(her) rejoice. May _____ look to You, Lord and to Your strength, may _____ seek Your face always. ~Amen

Psalm 4:8 Gracious God, let _____ lie down and sleep in peace. ~Amen

Psalm 37:40 Lord, when _____ is attacked by bullies or other evils, I pray that You, Lord, would help him(her), rescue him(her) from the wicked. Be _____'s shelter. ~Amen (NLT)

Proverbs 16:24 Lord God, may _____ use kind words, words that are like honey--sweet to the soul and healthy for the body. ~Amen (NLT)

Proverbs 16:28 Gracious God, I pray that _____ wouldn't participate in gossip or exclude his(her) peers, remind him(her) that a troublemaker plants seeds of strife, and a gossip separates the best of friends. ~Amen (NLT)

Isaiah 65:23b Lord, I pray that the Christians at _____ school will be a people blessed by You, they and their descendants. ~Amen

John
14:1

Lord, I pray the staff at _____ school will not let their hearts be troubled, but believe in You, God, and in Your Son Jesus Christ. ~Amen (NASB)

2 Corinthians
5:7

Dear God, may _____ be a person who walks by faith and not by sight. ~Amen

Galatians
6:9

Heavenly Father, let _____'s teacher and coaches not get tired of doing what is good. Help them not become discouraged and give up, but help them see that they will reap a harvest of blessing at the appropriate time. And, help _____ not to give up praying for their teachers and coaches. Amen (NLT)

Colossians
2:8

Heavenly Father, do not let any teacher take _____ captive through hollow and deceptive philosophy, which depends on human tradition and the basic principles of this world rather than on Christ. ~Amen

Titus
3:1-2

Heavenly Father, remind _____ to be subject to the rulers and authorities in his(her) life, to be obedient, to be ready to do whatever is good, and to slander no one (even if _____ doesn't agree with a decision made by a teacher/coach/parent). Prompt _____ to be peaceable and considerate and to show true humility toward everyone. ~Amen

Hebrews
13:17-18

Gracious God, cause _____ to obey his(her) leaders. Remind him(her) that they are accountable to You, God, and that he(she) should pray for them to live honorably. ~Amen (NLT)

Service

We were created to serve God and serve others. Pray that God will lead your child to serve.

Deuteronomy 10:12-13a
Lord God, I pray that You would show _____ what You require of him(her): may _____ fear You, Lord God, may _____ walk in all Your ways, may he(she) love You, and serve You Lord, with all his(her) heart and with all his(her) soul, and may _____ keep the commandments and statutes of the Lord. ~Amen

Matthew 5:10
Gracious God, bless _____ when he(she) is persecuted because of righteousness, those who persecuted will be given the kingdom of heaven. ~Amen

Matthew 20:26-28
Heavenly Father, teach _____ that if he(she) wants to become great, he(she) must be a servant. If _____ wants to be first, he(she) must be a slave-- just as the Son of Man did not come to be served, but to serve, and to give His life as a ransom for many. ~Amen

Ephesians 4:1-2
Lord, I pray for _____, that he(she) would walk in a manner worthy of You. Give _____ the humility and gentleness, along with the patience he(she) needs to bear with others in love. ~Amen (ESV)

Ephesians 4:11-16

Gracious God, You made some people apostles, some prophets, some evangelists, and some pastors and teachers. Show _____ where he(she) fits into Your divine arrangement, and let _____ use his(her) gifts to prepare Your people for works of service, so that the body of Christ may be built up in love. ~Amen

Ephesians 6:7-8

Gracious Father, I pray that You would motivate _____ to serve wholeheartedly, as if he(she) was serving You, not people; remind _____ that You will reward everyone for whatever good they do. ~Amen

Soul

Pray for your child's heart, desires and matters of the soul.

Numbers 32:23 — Heavenly Father, help _____ to keep his(her) word and not sin against You, Lord. If _____ fails to keep his(her) word, may his(her) sin be found out. ~Amen (NLT)

Deuteronomy 4:39 — Heavenly Father, may _____ acknowledge and take to heart that You are God in heaven above and on earth below. May he(she) believe that there is no other God but You. ~Amen

Joshua 24:15 — Holy Father, I pray that _____ would choose to say: As for me and my house, we will serve the Lord." (ESV)

2 Chronicles 7:14 — Heavenly Father, cause _____, who is called by Your name, to humble himself(herself) and pray, cause _____ to seek Your face and to turn from his(her) wicked ways, so that You will hear _____ and forgive his(her) sin. ~Amen

Psalm 19:13-14 — Father, may _____ offer You the sacrifice of a broken spirit; for a broken and repentant heart, O God, You will not despise. ~Amen (NLT)

Psalm 31:14-15 — Gracious Father, would You cause _____ to put his(her) trust in You, O Lord; let _____ say, "You are my God. My times and my days are in Your hands." ~Amen

Psalm 71:5	May You, O Sovereign Lord, be _____'s hope; may his(her) confidence be in You from childhood. ~Amen
Psalm 84:10	Heavenly Father, may _____ choose to be a doorkeeper to Your House, O Lord, than live the good life in the homes of the wicked. ~Amen (NLT)
Jeremiah 32:39-40	Heavenly Father, would You count _____ as one of Your people, and be his(her) God. Give _____ singleness of heart and action, so the he(she) will always fear You for his(her) own good and for the good of his(her) children. Make an everlasting covenant with _____. Never stop doing good to him(her), and inspire _____ to fear You so that he(she) will never turn away from You. ~Amen
Matthew 4:4	Heavenly Father, may _____ not live on bread alone, but on every Word that comes from the mouth of God. ~Amen
Matthew 5:3	God, would You bless _____ and help him(her) see his(her) need for You, for You promised that the Kingdom of Heaven will be given to him(her). ~Amen (NLT)
Matthew 6:13	Dear God, do not lead _____ into temptation but deliver him(her) from the evil one. ~Amen (NLT)
Matthew 22:37-39	Lord God, I pray that _____ would love You, Lord, with all his(her) heart, and with all his(her) soul, and with all his(her) mind. And help _____ to love his(her) neighbors as himself(herself). ~Amen

Acts 26:18	Gracious God, I pray that You would open _____'s eyes so they can see the difference between dark and light, and choose light, see the difference between Satan and God, and choose God. May they clearly see Your offer of sins forgiven, and choose a place in the family, in the company who begin real living by believing in You, Christ. ~Amen (MSG)
Romans 10:9	Gracious God, I pray that _____ would confess with his(her) mouth that Jesus is Lord, and believe in his(her) heart that You raised Jesus from the dead, so that he(she) will be saved. ~Amen (NLT)
Romans 12:2	Father God, may _____ not copy the behavior and customs of this world, instead, God, would You transform him(her) into a new person by changing the ways he(she) thinks. Help _____ know what You want him(her) to do, so that he(she) will know Your good and pleasing and perfect will. ~Amen (NLT)
Acts 26:18	Gracious God, I pray that you would open _____'s eyes so he(she) can see the difference between dark and light; may _____ choose light. Help _____ see the difference between Satan and God, and choose God. May he(she) clearly see Your offer of forgiveness of sins, and choose a place in the family, in the company of those who begin real living by believing in You, Christ. ~Amen (MSG)
2 Corinthians 6:14-17	Dear God, when _____'s dates, may he(she) not team up with those who are unbelievers. May _____ see that goodness cannot partner with wickedness, and light cannot live with darkness. Remind _____ that he(she) is a temple of the living God. ~Amen (NLT)

Philippians 2:13	Heavenly Father, remind _____, God, that You are working in him(her), and give _____ the desire and power to do what pleases You. ~Amen (NLT)
Philippians 3:8-9	Holy Father, I pray that _____ would consider everything else worthless as compared with the infinite value of knowing Christ Jesus as his(her) Lord. For Christ's sake, may _____ discard everything else, counting it all as garbage, so that he(she) can gain Christ and become one with Him. Help _____ no longer count on his(her) own righteousness through obeying the law but realize he(she) become righteous through faith in Christ. ~Amen (NLT)
1 Thessalonians 1:4-5	Lord, I ask that You choose _____. Bring the gospel to him(her) not just with words, but through power and Your Holy Spirit, so that _____ will be fully convinced of his(her) need of You, Lord. ~Amen
1 Thessalonians 5:23-24	Heavenly Father, You are the God of peace. Make _____ holy in every way. May his(her) whole spirit and soul and body be kept blameless until our Lord Jesus Christ comes again. Remind _____ that You are faithful. ~Amen (NLT)
1 Timothy 2:4-5	God, Your Word says that You want everyone to be saved and to understand the truth. May _____ know You as the only God and the One Mediator who can reconcile Himself with people. ~Amen (NLT)
Hebrews 4:12	Your Word, O God, is living and active, sharper than any double-edged sword, use it in _____'s life to penetrate to his(her) soul and spirit, joints and marrow; help _____ apply Your Word to judge the thoughts and attitudes of his(her) heart. ~Amen

Hebrews 11:6   Holy Father, I pray that _____ would understand
it impossible to please You apart from faith. May
he(she) come to You and believe that You exist and
know that You reward those who sincerely seek You.
~Amen (NLT)

**1 Peter
1:14-15**   Heavenly Father, I pray that _____ would live as
God's obedient child. Help him(her) live for You
and not satisfy his(her) own desires, but rather
help _____ to be holy in everything he(she) does.
~Amen (NLT)

**1 John
2:15**   All-powerful God, I pray that _____ would not
love the world's way, or love the world's goods. Help
him(her) see that love with the world squeezes out
love for You, Father. ~Amen (MSG)

**1 John
3:23**   Father, I pray that _____ will believe in the name of
Your Son Jesus Christ, and love others just as You
commanded him(her). ~Amen (NASB)

Temptation

Pray for your child to avoid temptation and grow in the things of God.

Deuteronomy 31:6
O God, I pray that _____ would be strong and take courage. Don't let him(her) be intimidated; don't let him(her) even give it a second thought because You, O God, are striding ahead of _____. You are right there with _____, remind him(her) You won't let him(her) down, You won't leave him(her). ~Amen (MSG)

1 Samuel 30:6b
Gracious God, may _____ be like David, and find his(her) strength in You, Lord God. ~Amen

Nehemiah 8:10b
Oh, God, may the joy of You, Lord, be _____'s strength. ~Amen

Psalm 10:4
Dear Lord, please guard _____ against pride that stops him(her) from seeking You out, Lord; in all _____'s thoughts help him(her) make room for You, God. ~Amen (Psalm 10:4)

Psalm 119:29-32
Heavenly Father, keep _____ from deceitful ways. Help him(her) to choose the way of truth and to set his(her) heart on Your laws, so that he(she) will not be put to shame. May _____ run in the path of Your commands, and may he(she) realize that You set his(her) heart free. ~Amen

Psalm 19:7-9
Lord, keep _____ from deliberate sins! Don't let sin control him(her). Instead, may the words of _____'s mouth and the thoughts of his(her) heart be pleasing to You, O Lord, the Rock, the Redeemer. ~Amen (NLT)

Proverbs **2:7-8**	Lord, I pray that You would be a shield to _____, help him(her) be upright and give him(her) victory. Guard _____'s course and protect his(her) way. ~Amen (NLT)
Romans **1:21-23**	O God, I pray as _____ takes his(her) faith as his(her) own You will protect him(her); may he(she) never refuse to glorify You as God, or fail to show You gratitude; keep _____'s thinking from becoming nonsense, don't let _____'s mind become senseless or darkened; keep him(her) from becoming a fool by claiming to be wise; never let _____ exchange Your glory, immortal God, for any false image. ~Amen (HSCB)
Romans **6:12-13**	Lord, I pray that _____ would not let sin control the way he(she) lives, give him(her) strength so as not to give in to sinful desires. Block _____ from using any part of his(her) body as an instrument of evil to serve sin. Instead, may _____ give him(herself) completely to God and bring glory to You, Lord. ~Amen (Romans 6:12-13 NLT)
Romans **12:1 &** **1 Corinthians** **6:18-20**	Dear Lord, help _____ to give his(her) body to You, God. May he(she) be a living and holy sacrifice. Help _____ to run away from sexual sin, remembering that his(her) body is a temple of the Holy Spirit. ~Amen (NLT)
Romans **16:19**	Heavenly Father, may _____ be wise as to what is good and innocent as to what is evil. ~Amen (ESV)
1 Corinthians **16:13**	Dear Lord, help _____ to be on guard, to stand firm in his(her) faith, to be a man(woman) of courage, and to be strong. Above all, help _____ do everything out of love. ~Amen

2 Corinthians 2:11	Holy Father, I pray that _____ will not unwittingly give Satan an opening for yet more mischief; help him(her) not be oblivious to his sly ways. ~Amen (MSG)
2 Corinthians 10:13	My Lord and God, because You are faithful, I ask that You not let _____ be tempted beyond what he(she) can bear, but when _____ is tempted, cause him(her) to look to You for the way out only You can provide, and give _____ strength to stand up under the stress of temptation. ~Amen
Galatians 5:1	Heavenly Father, remind _____ that Christ has really set him(her) free. Help _____ stay free, and not get tied up again in slavery to the law. ~Amen (NLT)
Galatians 5:19-22	Gracious God, give _____ strength to not follow the desires of his(her) sinful nature, but rather may _____ let the Holy Spirit control his(her) life; for the Holy Spirit will produce in him(her) love, joy, peace, patience, kindness, goodness, faithfulness, gentleness, and self-control. ~Amen (NLT)
Ephesians 5:10-14	Heavenly Father, may _____ carefully determine what pleases You, Lord. Block him(her) from taking part in the worthless deeds of evil and darkness; instead expose them. Shine Your light on any evil intentions of _____'s mind and expose them. Your light makes everything visible. ~Amen
Ephesians 6:9-10	God, I pray that _____ would be strong in You, Lord and in Your mighty power. May _____ put on the full armor of God so that he(she) can take a stand against the Devils' schemes. ~Amen

Ephesians 6:14	Holy, all-powerful God, I pray that You would enable _____ to stand firm with the belt of truth buckled around his(her) waist, with the breastplate of righteousness in place. ~Amen
2 Timothy 2:25-26	Heavenly Father, put people in _____'s life who will gently instruct him(her); and grant _____ repentance and lead him(her) to a knowledge of the Truth. Cause _____ to come to his(her) senses and escape the trap of the Devil, who has taken him(her) captive to do his will. ~Amen
Titus 2:6-8	Gracious God, may _____, as a young person, be self-controlled. Help _____ be an example to others by doing what is good; help _____ have integrity and soundness of speech. ~Amen (NLT)
Titus 2:11-12	God of Grace, reveal Your grace to _____. I pray that he(she) would do as Your Word instructs and turn from godless living and sinful pleasures. May _____ live in this evil world with wisdom, righteousness, and devotion to You, God. ~Amen (NLT)
Hebrews 12:10-11	Lord God, thank You for disciplining _____ so that he(she) might share in Your holiness. Use this discipline, which is not enjoyable while it is happening but painful to grow _____ in his(her) character and produce a peaceful harvest of right living. ~Amen (NLT)
James 1:22	Heavenly Father, I pray that _____ would realize that Your message is one to obey, not just to listen to. Show him(her) that by not obeying, he(she) is only fooling himself(herself). ~Amen

James **4:7-8**	Heavenly Father, I pray that You help _____ submit to You, O God, and to resist the devil. Make the devil flee from _____ as he(she) draws near to You. ~Amen
2 Peter **3:17-18**	Heavenly Father, I pray that _____ would be on guard so as not to be carried away by the errors of wicked people and possibly lose his(her) own secure footing. May _____ grow in grace and knowledge of the Lord and Savior Jesus Christ. ~Amen

Thanks

Pray for your child to be thankful.

Colossians 2:6-7 Heavenly Father, I pray that _____ would continue to live in Christ, rooted and built up in Him, strengthened in faith as he(she) was taught, and overflowing with thankfulness. ~Amen

1 Thessalonians 5:16-18 Heavenly Father, let _____ always be joyful. Let _____ keep on praying. No matter what happens, let _____ always be thankful, for this is God's will for him(her), and for those who belong to Christ Jesus. ~Amen (NLT)

Work Ethic

Pray for your child to work in all things as if unto the Lord.

Psalm **96:3**	Heavenly Father, I pray that You would help _____ develop a desire to see Your glory declared among the nations, Your marvelous works among all peoples. ~Amen (ESV)
Proverbs **6:9-1**	O God, some days I wonder how long _____ will laze around doing nothing, how long until he(she) gets out of bed. I pray that You show _____ that a nap here, a nap there, a day off here, a day off there can lead to a dirt-poor life, with poverty as his(her) permanent houseguest. ~Amen (MSG)
1 Corinthians **9:24-25**	Holy Father, remind _____ of the value of strict training. Help him(her) to run the race in such a way as to be the one who gets the prize. ~Amen (NLT)
1 Corinthians **15:58**	Dear God, I pray during _____'s life, he(she) would be strong and immovable, always working enthusiastically for You Lord, knowing that nothing he(she) does for You is ever useless. ~Amen (NLT)
Galatians **6:5**	Heavenly Father, I pray that _____ would learn responsibility and how to carry him(her) own load. ~Amen (HCSB)
Colossians **3:20-21**	Heavenly Father, teach _____ to obey us (his/her parents) in everything, for this pleases You, Lord. Do not let us do or say anything that would embitter or discourage _____. ~Amen
Colossians **3:23-24**	Holy Father, may _____ work willingly at whatever he(she) does, as though working for the Lord rather than for people. Help _____ remember that the Master he(she) is serving is Christ. ~Amen (NLT)

Section 3
Bible Blessings

We don't "bless" people very much. But we should, don't you think? After all, who doesn't want to be blessed? Who wouldn't want a reminder of who they are spoken to them and prayed over them?

We all want to be blessed. You want to be blessed. I want to be blessed. And so do our kids. They want to be blessed. They need to be blessed. What better way to bless them, than using the words God used in His Word?

These 43 blessings (and there could be hundreds more) are listed here in the order you will find them in the Bible. All of them are adapted from the NIV. If you prefer another translation, simply use the Scripture reference and create your own!

Use these blessings first thing in the morning. Or as you tuck your kids in at night. Or as they head out the door to school or work. Or while they eat breakfast. Or tape one to their bathroom mirror. Or put one on the dashboard of their car. Or slide one into their lunchbox. Or…

The Blessings

From Deuteronomy 6:24-26

Blessing:_____ I pray that God will richly bless you and keep you. May the Lord make his face shine on you and be gracious to you. May the Lord turn his face toward you and give you peace.

From Psalm 37:4

Blessing: _____, may you always delight yourself in the Lord. Then he will give you the desires of your heart.

From Proverbs 3:5-6

Blessing: _____, Trust in the Lord with all your heart and lean not on your own understanding; in all your ways submit to him, and he will make your paths straight.

From Jeremiah 29:11

Blessing: _____, the Lord declares that he knows the plans he has for you. They are plans to prosper you and not to harm you. They are plans to give you hope and a future.

From Romans 8:14-17

Blessing: _____ , always remember that you are led by the Sprit of God and are therefore a child of God. The Spirit you received does not make a slave, so there is no need to live in fear. Rather, the Spirit you received brought about your adoption to sonship. By him we cry "Abba, Father." The Spirit himself testifies with your spirit that you are God's child. Now if you are a child, then you are an heir – an heir of God and co-heir with Christ, if indeed you share in his sufferings in order that you may also share in his glory.

From Romans 8:26-27

Blessing: _____, the Spirit is there to help you in your weakness. Even when you do not know what you ought to pray for, the Spirit himself intercedes for you with groanings to deep for words. And remember, he who searches hearts knows the mind of the Spirit, because the Spirit intercedes for God's people in accordance with the will of God.

From Romans 8:28-30

Blessing: _____, be confident and know that in all things God works for the good of those who love him, who have been called according to his purpose. For those God foreknew he also predestined to be conformed to the image of his Son, that he might be the firstborn among many brothers and sisters. And those he predestined, he also called; those he called, he also justified. Those he justified, he also glorified.

From Romans 8: 31-35, 37-39

Blessing: _____ God is for you. Who can be against you? He did not spare his own Son, but gave him up for you. How will he not, along with Jesus, graciously give you all things? Who will bring any charge against you, since you are chosen by God? God is the one who justifies. Who then is the one who condemns. No one. Christ Jesus who died – more that that, who was raised to life – is at the right hand of God and is also interceding for you. Who share separate you from the love of Christ? Shall trouble or hardship or persecution or famine or nakedness or danger or sword? No. In all these things you are more than a conqueror through him how loved you. I am convinced that neither death nor life, neither angels nor demons, neither the present nor the future, nor any powers, neither height nor depth, nor anything else in all creation, will be able to separate you from the love of God that is in Christ Jesus our Lord.

From Romans 15:4-6

Blessing: _____, everything that was written in the past was written to teach us, so that through the endurance taught in the Scriptures and the encouragement they provide we might have hope. May the God who gives endurance and encouragement give you the same attitude of mind toward each other that Christ Jesus had, so that with one mind and one voice you may glorify the God and Father of our Lord Jesus Christ.

From Romans 15:13

Blessing: _____, I pray the God of hope, would fill you with all joy and peace as you trust in him, so that you may overflow with hope by the power of the Holy Spirit.

From 1 Corinthians 1:7-9

Blessing: _____, you do not lack any spiritual gift as you eagerly wait for our Lord Jesus Christ to be revealed. He will also keep you firm to the end, so that you will be blameless on the day of our Lord Jesus Christ. God is faithful, who has called you into fellowship with his Son, Jesus Christ our Lord.

From 1 Corinthians 10:13

Blessing: ____, whenever you are tempted, remember that no temptation has overtaken you except what is common to mankind. And God is faithful; he will not let you be tempted beyond what you can bear. But when you are tempted, he will also provide a way out so that you can endure it.

From 2 Corinthians 2:14

Blessing: _____, may you give thanks to God, who always leads us as captives in Christ's triumphal procession. He is using you to spread the aroma of the knowledge of Christ everywhere.

From 2 Corinthians 3:16-18

Blessing: _____, since you have turned to the Lord, the veil that covers your heart is taken away. The Lord is the Spirit, and where the Spirit of the Lord is, there is freedom. You, along with all Jesus-followers, contemplate the Lord's glory with unveiled faces. You are being transformed into his image with ever-increasing glory, which comes from the Lord, who is the Spirit.

From 2 Corinthians 4:16-18

Blessing: _____, do not lose heart. Outwardly, you may be wasting away, but inwardly you are being renewed day by day. Your light and momentary troubles are achieving for you an eternal glory that far outweighs them all. So fix your eyes not on what is seen, but on what is unseen, since what is seen is temporary, but what is unseen is eternal.

From 2 Corinthians 5:17-21

Blessing: _____, you are in Christ, so you are a new creation. The old has gone, the new is here! All this is from God. All this is from God, who reconciled you to himself through Christ and gave you the ministry of reconciliation: that God was reconciling the world to himself in Christ, not counting people's sins against them. And he has committed to you the message of reconciliation. You are therefore Christ's ambassador, as though God were making his appeal through you. We implore you on Christ's behalf: Be reconciled to God. God made him who had no sin to be sin for us, so that in him you might become the righteousness of God.

From 2 Corinthians 9:6-8

Blessing: _____, remember that whoever sows sparingly will also reap sparingly, and whoever sows generously will also reap generously. You should give what you have decided in your heart to give, not reluctantly or under compulsion, for God loves a cheerful giver. And God is able to bless you abundantly, so that in all things at all times, having all that you need, you will abound in every good work.

From 2 Corinthians 12:9-10

Blessing: _____, the Lord says, "My grace is sufficient for you, for my power is made perfect in weakness." So when you boast, boast about your weaknesses, so that Christ's power may rest on you. For Christ's sake, delight in weaknesses, in insults, in hardships, in persecutions, in difficulties. For when you are weak, then you are strong.

From Galatians 5:22-25

Blessing: _____, may you be filled with the fruit of the Spirit. May you be filled to overflowing with love, joy, peace, patience, kindness, goodness, faithfulness, gentleness, and self-control; knowing that against such things there is no law. May you remember today that you belong to Christ Jesus and have crucified the flesh with its passions and desires. May you live by the Spirit, and keep in step with the Spirit.

From Ephesians 1:3-8

Blessing: _____, God the Father has blessed you in the heavenly realms with every spiritual blessing in Christ. You were chosen in him before the creation of the world to be holy and blameless in his sight. In love he predestined you for adoption to sonship through Jesus Christ. This was in accordance with his pleasure and his will, and it was to the praise of his glorious grace which he has freely giving us in the One he loves. You have redemption through his blood, the forgiveness of sins, in accordance with the riches of God's grace that he lavished on you.

From Ephesians 3:16-21

Blessing: _____, I pray that out of his glorious riches he may strengthen you with power through his Spirit in your inner being, so that Christ may dwell in your heart through faith. And I pray that you, being rooted and established in love, may have power, together with all the Lord's holy people, to grasp how wide and long and high and deep is the love of Christ, and to know this love that surpasses knowledge—that you may be filled to the measure of all the fullness of God. Now to him who is able to do immeasurably more than all you could ask or imagine, according to his power that is at work within you, to him be glory in the church, in you, and in Christ Jesus throughout all generations, for ever and ever! Amen.

From Ephesians 5:1

Blessing:_____, follow God's example, as a dearly loved child, and walk in the way of love, just as Christ loved you and gave himself up for you as a fragrant offering and sacrifice to God.

From Ephesians 5:8

Blessing: _____, before you gave your life to Christ, you were once darkness, but now you are light in the Lord. Live as a child of light.

From Ephesians 6:10-18

Blessing:: _____, be strong in the Lord and in his mighty power. Put on the full armor of God, so that you can take your stand against the devil's schemes. Remember that your struggle is not against flesh and blood, but against the rulers, against the authorities, against the powers of this dark world and against the spiritual forces of evil in the heavenly realms. Therefore put on the full armor of God, so that when the day of evil comes, you may be able to stand your ground, and after you have done everything, to stand. Stand firm then, with the belt of truth buckled around your waist, with the breastplate of righteousness in place, and with your feet fitted with the readiness that comes from the gospel of peace. In addition to all this, take up the shield of faith, with which you can extinguish all the flaming arrows of the evil one. Take the helmet of salvation and the sword of the Spirit, which is the word of God. And pray in the Spirit on all occasions with all kinds of prayers and requests. With this in mind, be alert and always keep on praying for all the Lord's people.

From Philippians 1: 9-11

Blessing: _____, I pray that your love may abound more and more in knowledge and depth of insight, so that you may be able to discern what is best and may be pure and blameless for the day of Christ, filled with the fruit of righteousness that comes through Jesus Christ, to the glory and praise of God.

From Philippians 4:4-7

Blessing: _____, may you rejoice in the Lord always. I will say it again: Rejoice! Let your gentleness be evident to all. The Lord is near. Do not be anxious about anything, but in every situation, by prayer and petition, with thanksgiving, present your requests to God. And the peace of God, which transcends all understanding, will guard your heart and your mind in Christ Jesus.

From Philippians 4:8-9

Blessing: _____, whatever is true, whatever is noble, whatever is right, whatever is pure, whatever is lovely, whatever is admirable—if anything is excellent or praiseworthy—think about such things. Whatever you have learned or received or heard from me, or seen in me—put it into practice. And the God of peace will be with you.

From Colossians 1:9-14

Blessing:_____, since the day I heard about you, I have not stopped praying for you. I continually ask God to fill you with the knowledge of his will through all the wisdom and understanding that the Spirit gives, so that you may live a life worthy of the Lord and please him in every way: bearing fruit in every good work, growing in the knowledge of God, being strengthened with all power according to his glorious might so that you may have great endurance and patience, and giving joyful thanks to the Father, who has qualified you to share in the inheritance of his holy people in the kingdom of light. For he has rescued you from the dominion of darkness and brought you into the kingdom of the Son he loves, in whom you have redemption, the forgiveness of sins.

From Colossians 2:6-10

Blessing: _____, just as you received Christ Jesus as Lord, continue to live your life in him, rooted and built up in him, strengthened in the faith as you were taught, and overflowing with thankfulness. See to it that no one takes you captive through hollow and deceptive philosophy, which depends on human tradition and the elemental spiritual forces of this world rather than on Christ. For in Christ all the fullness of the Deity lives in bodily form, and in Christ you have been brought to fullness.

From Colossians 3:1-4

Blessing:_____, Since, then, you have been raised with Christ, set your hearts on things above, where Christ is, seated at the right hand of God. Set your minds on things above, not on earthly things. For you died, and your life is now hidden with Christ in God. When Christ, who is your life, appears, then you also will appear with him in glory.

From 2 Thessalonians 1:11-12

Blessing: _____, I constantly pray for you! I pray that our God may make you worthy of his calling, and that by his power he may bring to fruition your every desire for goodness and your every deed prompted by faith. I pray this so that the name of our Lord Jesus may be glorified in you, and you in him, according to the grace of our God and the Lord Jesus Christ.

From 2 Thessalonians 2:15-16

Blessing: _____, may you stand firm and hold fast to the teaching we passed on to you. May our Lord Jesus Christ himself and God our Father, who loved you and by his grace gave you eternal encouragement and good hope, encourage your heart and strengthen you in every good deed and word.

From 2 Thessalonians 3:5

Blessing: _____, may the Lord direct your heart into God's love and Christ's perseverance.

From 2 Thessalonians 3:16 & 18

Blessing: _____, now may the Lord of peace himself give you peace at all times and in every way. The Lord be with you and may the grace of our Lord Jesus Christ be with you.

From 1 Timothy 4:12

Blessing: _____, don't let anyone look down on you because you are young, but set an example for the believers in speech, in conduct, in love, in faith and in purity.

From 2 Timothy 1:7-10

Blessing: _____, the Spirit God gave you does not make you timid, but gives you power, love and self-discipline. So do not be ashamed of the testimony about our Lord or of me his prisoner. Rather, join with me in suffering for the gospel, by the power of God. He has saved you and called you to a holy life—not because of anything you have done but because of his own purpose and grace. This grace was given you in Christ Jesus before the beginning of time, but it has now been revealed through the appearing of our Savior, Christ Jesus, who has destroyed death and has brought life and immortality to light through the gospel.

From 2 Timothy 4:18

Blessing: _____, may you be reminded every day that the Lord will rescue you from every evil attack and will bring you safely to his heavenly kingdom. To him be glory for ever and ever. Amen.

From Hebrews 13:20-21

Blessing: _____, now may the God of peace, who through the blood of the eternal covenant brought back from the dead our Lord Jesus, that great Shepherd of the sheep, equip you with everything good for doing his will, and may he work in you what is pleasing to him, through Jesus Christ, to whom be glory for ever and ever. Amen.

From 1 Peter 1:3-5

Blessing: _____, praise be to the God and Father of our Lord Jesus Christ! In his great mercy he has given you new birth into a living hope through the resurrection of Jesus Christ from the dead, and into an inheritance that can never perish, spoil or fade. This inheritance is kept in heaven for you, who through faith are shielded by God's power until the coming of the salvation that is ready to be revealed in the last time.

From 1 Peter 1:22-25

Blessing: _____, now that you have purified yourself by obeying the truth so that you have sincere love for others, love others deeply, from the heart. For you have been born again, not of perishable seed, but of imperishable, through the living and enduring word of God.

Remember, "All people are like grass, and all their glory is like the flowers of the field; the grass withers and the flowers fall, but the word of the Lord endures forever." And this is the word that was preached to you.

From 1 Peter 2:9-10

Blessing: _____, always remember that as a member of God's family, you are one of a chosen people, a royal priesthood, a holy nation, God's special possession, that you may declare the praises of him who called you out of darkness into his wonderful light. Once you were not a people, but now you are the people of God; once you had not received mercy, but now you have received mercy.

From 2 Peter 1:3-8

Blessing: _____, God's divine power has given you everything you need for a godly life through your knowledge of him who called you by his own glory and goodness. Through these he has given you his very great and precious promises, so that through them you may participate in the divine nature, having escaped the corruption in the world caused by evil desires. For this very reason, make every effort to add to your faith goodness; and to goodness, knowledge; and to knowledge, self-control; and to self-control, perseverance; and to perseverance, godliness; and to godliness, mutual affection; and to mutual affection, love. For if you possess these qualities in increasing measure, they will keep you from being ineffective and unproductive in your knowledge of our Lord Jesus Christ.

From 1 John 2:14

Blessing: _____, you, dear child, know the Father. You are strong, the word of God lives in your, and you have overcome the evil one.

About the Authors

Keith Ferrin is an author, speaker, storyteller, and blogger. Actually, that's more of what he "does." As far as who he is…He is a disciple of Jesus Christ, a husband to Kari (world's most outstanding wife), and a father to Sarah, Caleb, and Hannah (the three coolest – and craziest – kids on the planet). Keith is also a coffee drinker, ice cream eater, youth soccer coach (who occasionally makes the mistake of thinking his body can still do what it did when he was 17), amateur guitar player, lover of twisty-turny movies, and eater of almost any kind of food (except olives). You can find Keith in Seattle where he is the happy guy hanging out with his wife and kids doing something fun in the outdoors. You can also catch him online at KeithFerrin.com.

Judy Fetzer is an organizer, event planner, and resource woman extraordinaire. She puts those skills into practice as executive assistant to the Provost at Northwest University. Judy can often be found creating a new quilt, exploring new neighborhoods with walking companion Copper the Goldendoodle, and tending to her flower beds. Her favorite activity is connecting with people -- through book club, a "day of adventure," Bible study groups, and soul deep conversations. Judy and her husband Barry have three children, all grown up; they continue to receive the blessing of prayer from their "mother hen." Find her at www.mamahenprays.wordpress.com.

Made in the USA
San Bernardino, CA
25 July 2017